Over 100 delicious recipes

Italian

DUMONT
monte

Table of Contents

1. Introduction

Italy keeps fascinating us again and again with its unique culture, its breathtaking landscape, its warm and family-oriented mentality and last but not least its simple yet spectacular cuisine. If you ever had the chance to experience Italian hospitality with an Italian family you will never forget it. Simple dishes, such as spaghetti with tomato sauce or delicious crostini turn into culinary highlights if they are prepared with love, patience and care and eaten in a relaxed fun atmosphere.

The geographic shape of this long peninsula fostered the development of very different dishes in the individual regions yet all dishes are similar in one aspect: their fascinating simplicity, nurtured by the freshness and quality of its ingredients.

Northern and Southern Italy make pasta dishes in all varieties, the best risotti, wonderful fish and meat dishes and of course many irresistible dolce! You can prepare all these tempting treats at home very easily. Let our recipes entice you to take a culinary journey through Italy!

Italian cuisine is not only varied and delicious, it is extremely healthy and therefore recommended for everyone who follows a nutritious diet. Ingredients like olive oil, fish, vegetables, fruit and fresh herbs are especially valuable for our nutrition. Sun-ripened vegetables and fruits are filled to the brim with vitamins and minerals. Freshly squeezed olive oil supplies our body with necessary unsaturated fatty acids like linolenic acid. Add the uncomplicated and careful preparation of the dishes and your enjoyment of them. Everything is cooked as naturally as possible and enjoyed peacefully and without any hurry. That's the Italian way.

As a starter one eats a little antipasto or a small salad to slowly tune the stomach up for the meal. Then a light pasta or a risotto. The size of the meat or fish course seems more of a side dish than a main course. Small portions of different things mean more enjoyment and easier digestion. After all, one does not eat to fill up but rather to feel good afterwards.

Italy has the most vineyards anywhere in the world and is the top wine producer world wide.

In bella Italia, wine was never a luxury, it is considered food like bread, olive oil and tomatoes. And to this day, a meal without vino is unthinkable for most Italians. Wine is the common beverage with a meal and not like in other cultures a beverage one enjoys socially when getting together with friends. This seems spartan, but in Italy meals take a much longer time than here.

Local wine from the surrounding hills is preferred and it usually harmonizes very well with the specialties of the respective region. Italians are traditionalists and stick with products from their country.

Antipasti are served with a young and fruity white wine, pasta dishes taste best with not too tannin rich red wines, and for the meat course a strong red is recommended. At the end of a good meal Italians love a good espresso or grappa.

Buon appetito e salute!

2. Kitchen Tools and Equipment

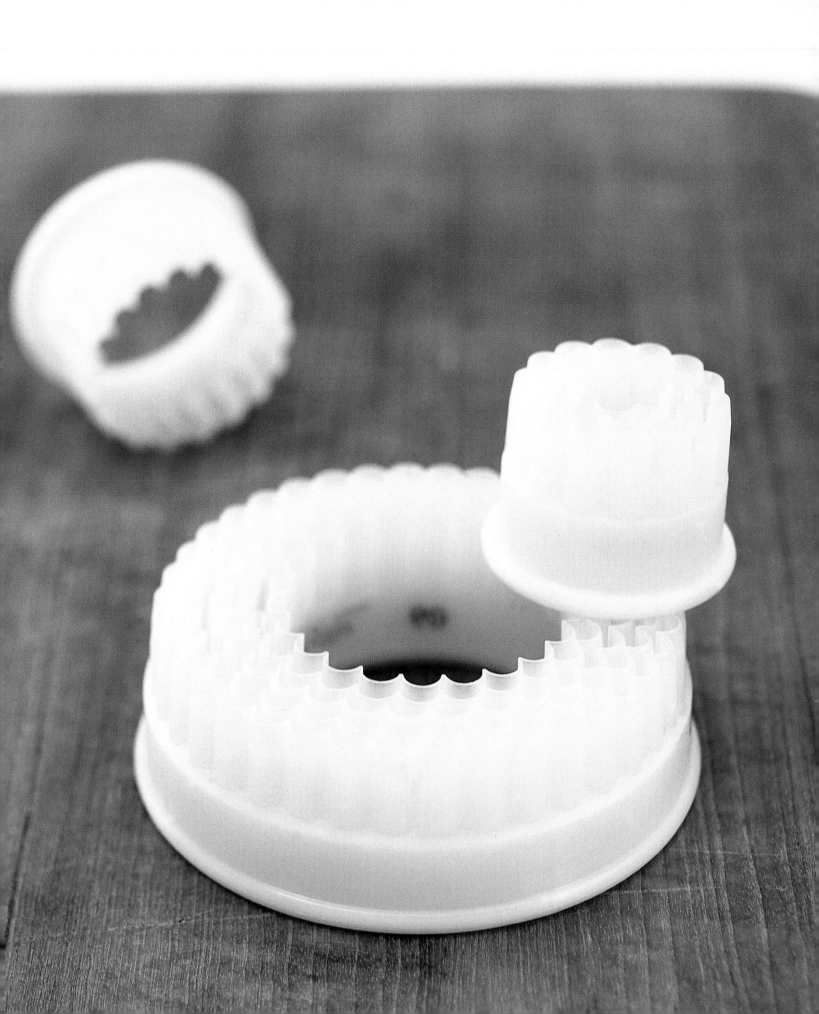

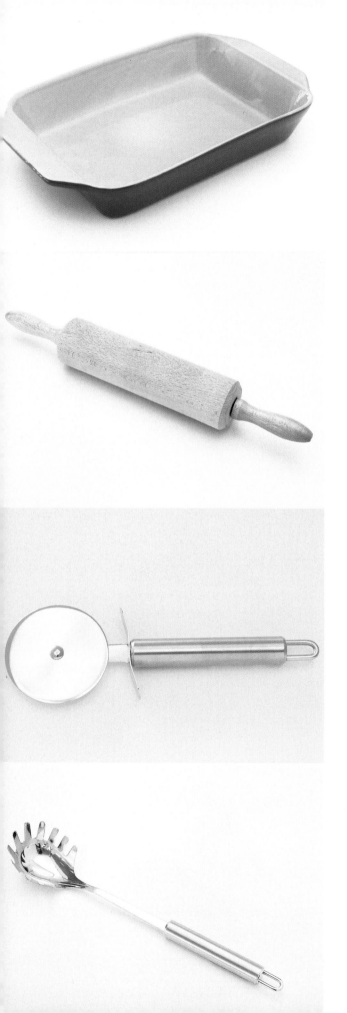

Lasagne dish

A must for vegetable or meat casserole dishes. Ingredients for lasagne or moussaka are layered into the oven-proof dish and baked in the oven. It is best to serve the food in the dish so it keeps warm.

Rolling pin

All firm doughs, e.g. cookie dough, yeast dough or pasta dough, can be rolled out with a rolling pin to the desired size and thickness. It is important to apply even pressure with both hands.

Pizza cutter

Cheese crust or crispy dough edge - this little sharp pizza wheel easily cuts any pizza into even pieces.

Spaghetti server

Its practical teeth allow a secure grip on the pasta. Spaghetti, penne or linguine can easily be divided into individual portions.

Ravioli cutter

If you do not have a ravioli cutter you can use regular cookie cutters.

Mortar and pestle

For crushing and grinding spices, e.g. pepper corns, juniper berries, cloves or to prepare pesto.

Pasta machine

Used for freshly prepared home-made pasta, e.g. lasagne sheets, ravioli, fettucine and spaghetti. It is so easy to handle that even kitchen novices can prepare delicious pasta.

Parmesan grater

With this easy kitchen tool you can grate parmesan cheese in no time. Of course, other types of hard cheese can also be grated. Just set cheese grater on the table so your guests can help themselves.

3. Italy in our Kitchen

Pasta dough

Basic recipe:
400 g flour
200 g wheat semolina
3 eggs
6 egg yolks
2 tablespoons oil
A pinch of salt

Mix flour and remaining ingredients together and knead into a smooth dough. The oil makes the dough workable, so it can easily be rolled out. Wrap pasta dough in clingfilm and allow to rest for about 1 hour.

Green Pasta Dough

For green pasta dough - also called spinach pasta - knead finely puréed spinach and the ingredients of the basic pasta recipe into a smooth dough.

For the spinach mixture cook about 500 g cleaned spinach (650 g before cleaning) in plenty of salted water for 8 minutes. Drain in a colander and squeeze dry thoroughly. Finely purée dry spinach in food processor and knead into a smooth dough with flour, semolina, eggs, egg yolks, oil and salt. Add some flour if necessary. Wrap green pasta dough in clingfilm and allow to rest for about 1 hour.

Ravioli

This popular pasta shape can be stuffed with a wide variety of fillings: meat, poultry, fish or vegetable fillings. Shaping ravioli takes some practice and patience but the beautiful and delicious result makes all the effort worthwhile.

Step 1

Prepare pasta dough (see page 22) and roll out thinly with a pasta machine. It is important to pass the dough through the pasta machine a few times. Keep dusting pasta sheets with flour, fold up and pass through pasta machine again. This is the only way to achieve the desired consistency of the pasta sheets.

For the filling, blanch 500 g spinach in boiling salted water (makes about 180 g), rinse under ice cold water, squeeze dry and chop finely.

Mix spinach with 500 g ricotta cheese and 2 finely chopped garlic cloves. Season mixture with salt, pepper and freshly grated nutmeg.

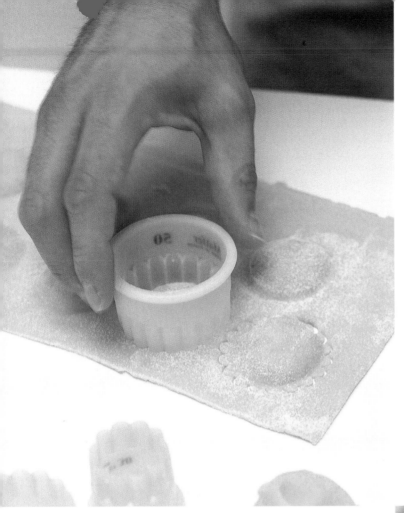

Step 4

Use a round or square cutter to cut out ravioli and dust with flour until further use. If you do not have a cutter handy, cut out ravioli with a pastry wheel cutter or a smooth knife. Cook ready ravioli in boiling salted water for about 4-5 minutes, carefully remove with a skimmer and serve with sage butter and freshly grated parmesan cheese or tomato sauce.

Step 2

Fill ricotta-spinach stuffing into piping bag with a tip and pipe small dollops onto pasta sheet, 5 cm apart. Whisk egg yolk with a few drops of water and thinly brush onto edges using a brush.

Step 3

Cover with second pasta sheet and pinch edges together tightly.

Ravioli

It is best to only use very fine fillings for ravioli, e.g. spinach-ricotta-filling or a tender meat or fish filling. Ravioli should be eaten right after preparation if possible. Since the dough sheets are very thin, they soften easily and then lose their shape. Place in boiling salted water, wait for them to rise to the top and remove pot from heat. The cooking time depends on the size of the ravioli – small ravioli take about 2 minutes, larger ones 5-7 minutes.

Tortelloni

This pasta shape looks like a bishop's mitre and is very beautiful to look at. Dry tortelloni slightly after preparation on a floured surface, and cook in rolling boiling salted water for about 5 minutes. Tortelloni with lamb filling and spicy eggplant sauce taste delicious.

Tortellini

This small stuffed pasta can be served in a strong broth or as a hot appetizer. For the meat filling , e.g. sauté mixed chopped meat until crumbly and season with rosemary and thyme. Allow mixture to cool, bind with egg yolk and stuff tortellini with mixture. Cook in rolling boiling salted water over high heat, depending on size, for about 5 minutes.

Cannelloni

These filled dough tubes can be prepared with white or green pasta dough. The rolls can be filled as desired: Pork, lamb or beef are just as suitable as chicken or turkey. They can also be stuffed with pike or pike-perch mousse. Fish cannelloni are complemented best by a champagne or mustard sauce. Cannelloni can easily be prepared in advance. Bake shortly before serving, in preheated oven at 180 °C for about 20 minutes, depending on filling.

Pesto

This popular cold sauce goes
best with spaghetti. It can
also be served with sautéed
meat, e.g. lamb cutlets or
small veal schnitzel. Stored
in a tightly closed jar, pesto
keeps in the refrigerator for
several days.

Ingredients

1 bunch of basil, 1 sprig of thyme, 2 garlic cloves, 2 tablespoons roasted pine nuts, 6 tablespoons freshly grated parmesan cheese, 200 ml olive oil, salt and freshly ground black pepper.

Pluck basil and thyme leaves, peel garlic cloves and finely crush with pine nuts with mortar and pestle. Slowly stir in parmesan cheese and oil and season with salt and pepper. If you do not have mortar and pestle, you can also use a hand blender to crush ingredients.

4. Spices and Other Ingredients

Mustard-Pickled Fruits

Fruits like cherries, plums, peaches, figs, mirabelles and pears are preserved with sugar, glucose syrup, water and mustard oil. They taste spicy and can be served with poultry or meat dishes.

Mozzarella

This popular soft cheese with its slightly sour taste was originally prepared from buffalo milk. It is generally sold in stores packaged in brine. Mozzarella tastes best cold with tomatoes, olive oil and fresh basil. But this fairly neutral tasting cheese can also be used as a topping on casserole dishes or pizzas.

Parmesan Cheese

This hard cheese made from cows' milk is a classic ingredient of Italian cuisine. Parmesan cheese is known for its strong flavour. Freshly grated, it adds a final touch to pasta or risotto. Gourmets love to savour small pieces of parmesan cheese drizzled with olive oil with fresh baguette and a glass of red wine.

Peperoncini

These little red "devils" can be purchased fresh or dried. They add a nice spiciness to dishes. The hot parts of the fruit are the seeds. If you have a sensitive palate, remove seeds from fresh peperoncinis and use only the pulp.

Sage

Fresh sage is used a lot in Italian cuisine– sautéed in butter with gnocchi or as a spice for veal, poultry or fish. Sage can be recognised by its longish, hairy leaves, which have a strong smell and a flavourful taste.

Oregano

Also called "wild marjoram". Dried on pizza or fresh in tomato sauce – oregano adds its own, very specific taste to everything. It is also loved as a seasoning for potato dishes.

Rosemary

Green rosemary needles play an important role in Mediterranean cuisine. It does not matter - fish, meat, vegetables or potatoes, rosemary generally adds a very special Mediterranean flavour to any dish. When freshly harvested from the rosemary bush its flavour is most intense and you should be careful with the dosage. Too much rosemary can overpower the natural taste of the other ingredients. In combination with thyme, rosemary is unbeatable.

Basil

The number one herb among those used fresh are the flavourful leaves of this annual. They add the finishing touch to salads as well as any Mediterranean dish. Basil is a must for all tomato dishes. We recommend always keeping a basil plant growing on your window sill or in the garden.

Pine Nuts

These oily, flavourful oval seeds are not cheap, but worth every penny. The taste of classic pesto with pine nuts is incomparable. Spicy or sweet – dishes with pine nuts are always a special treat. When roasting pine nuts in a pan you don't need any oil. The seeds contain enough fat of their own. Roasting intensifies their flavour.

Raisins

Italian cuisine uses these air-dried grapes not only in desserts. Veal liver with raisins and pine nuts, for example, is a dish that combines sweet and sour tastes. The natural sweetness of raisins also goes very well with fish. It is best to soak raisins in lukewarm black tea. Depending upon the dish, cognac, Calvados or rum adds additional flavour to the raisins.

Eggplant

In order to lighten their bitter taste, sprinkle eggplants with salt, allow to "sweat" and squeeze dry. With newer strains this is no longer necessary since they are cultivated in such a way that there is hardly any bitter taste left. Eggplants need to have a smooth, shiny skin. It is not good to store them for too long and at temperatures below 5°C the skin becomes blemished. In addition to the well-known purple eggplants, well stocked stores carry yellow and white eggplants most of which are round. But apart from the visual difference, they taste pretty much the same.

5. Stocks, Sauces and Vinaigrettes

Seafood Stock

It pays to keep some seafood stock in the freezer for emergencies. It can be used in many different ways, e.g. for soups, sauces or as a finishing touch for pasta dishes with fish.

❶ Chop carrots, celery and shallots into coarse cubes. Also chop leek into coarse cubes and set aside.

❷ Dry seafood shells in the oven at 100 °C for about 2 hours. Finely chop shells and briefly sauté in hot butter over low heat for about 5 minutes. Add carrots, celery, shallots, garlic and tomato paste and sauté for an additional 5 minutes.

❸ Add herbs and spices, briefly sauté with the other ingredients and pour in white wine and port wine. Add leek and season with coarse sea salt.

❹ Add water or fish stock and simmer uncovered over low heat for about 35 minutes.

❺ Strain stock through a fine-mesh sieve.

❻ Seafood stock keeps well in the refrigerator for a few days. It can also be divided into individual portions and frozen.

Makes 1 l stock

2 carrots, peeled
1/2 celery root, peeled
3 shallots, peeled
1 stalk leek, peeled
   (only use white part)
1 kg shells of scampi and
   crayfishes
50 g unsalted butter
3 garlic cloves, unpeeled
   and pressed
1 tablespoon tomato paste
3 bay leaves
2 sprigs of thyme
4 sprigs of dill
4 sprigs of parsley
1/2 teaspoon fennel seeds
100 ml white wine
5 cl white Port wine
Coarse sea salt
1.5 l water or fish stock

Tuna Sauce

2 shallots, peeled and diced

1 tablespoon olive oil

6 anchovies

1 1/2 tablespoons capers,
  chopped

2 cans of tuna in oil

4 tablespoons mayonnaise

50 g liquid cream

50 ml dry white wine

1 lemon for garnish

Salt

Sugar

Freshly ground white pepper

1 tablespoon chopped parsley

Classic Italian cuisine without vitello tonnato, this tempting combination of meat and fish? Unthinkable. Slowly bake veal in the oven, leave to cool, slice thinly and serve with tuna sauce and fresh lemon. Tuna sauce can easily be prepared in advance since it keeps in the refrigerator for 2-3 days. So you magically have a delicious dinner ready in no time. It also tastes good by itself as a dip for vegetable sticks or as an aperitif with fresh baguette.

❶ Sauté shallots in olive oil until soft and translucent, add anchovies and capers, season with salt and pepper and leave to cool.

❷ Drain tuna pieces in a colander. Mix with mayonnaise, cream, white wine and cooled onion mixture and finely purée using a hand blender. Season with salt, pepper and a pinch of sugar. Finish with parsley.

Serves 4

Walnut–Honey Sauce

80 g mixed mustard-pickled
  fruits, diced

80 g walnuts, chopped

1 tablespoon almonds, chopped

2 tablespoons honey

2 tablespoons grated baguette

3 tablespoons juice from
  mustard-pickled fruits

Salt

Freshly ground black pepper

This combination of spiciness, sweetness and nut flavour tastes especially good with braised meat or grilled fish.

❶ Mix diced pickled fruits with walnuts, almonds, honey and grated baguette. Stir in pickled fruit juice and season with salt and pepper.

Serves 4

Poultry Stock

1 kg poultry bones

1 onion, peeled

Vegetables for making soup
    (e.g. carrots, leeks, celery)

2 sprigs of thyme

Some orange and lemon peel,
    organically grown

1/4 l white wine

2 cloves

1 bay leaf

5 black peppercorns

Salt

To make poultry stock it is best to use chicken bones, but turkey bones can be used as well. For game dishes it is best to use a stock made from guinea fowl, duck or wild duck. To intensify the taste, sauté poultry pieces in oil first, then pour in liquid.

❶ Clean poultry bones under cold running water and drain. Place in stock pot with 1 l cold water and bring to a boil. Add vegetables, herbs, orange and lemon peel and spices.

❷ Add white wine and simmer slowly for about 1 hour. Strain through a fine-mesh sieve and salt lightly.

Makes 3/4 l stock

Fish Stock

1 kg fish trimmings

1 onion, peeled

1/2 fennel bulb

2 stalks celery with leaves

1 clove garlic, unpeeled
    and pressed

1 teaspoon unsalted butter

100 ml dry white wine

1 l water

1 sprig of thyme

1 bay leaf

10 white peppercorns, crushed

Coarse sea salt

It is best to use trimmings only from white fish, so the stock stays clear and has a neutral taste.

❶ Soak fish trimmings for 1/2 hour to wash away any remaining blood completely– this will prevent the stock from turning cloudy. Wash and dice vegetables and briefly sauté in butter over low heat, so vegetables do not burn. Add drained fish trimmings, white wine and water. Add herbs and spices and slowly bring to a boil.

❷ Simmer gently for about 30 minutes, skimming off any foam that rises to the surface from time to time. Strain stock through a fine-mesh sieve and use for making soup or sauces.

Makes 3/4 l stock

Saint Stefano Vinaigrette

This fancy marinade charms you with its spicy sweetness and goes very well with sautéed or grilled meat, fish and poultry. A special treat are anchovies marinated with this vinaigrette until they are completely soaked with the sauce.

❶ Roast pine nuts in skillet without oil until golden brown. Allow to cool slightly and chop coarsely. Finely chop capers and raisins and mix with olive oil.

❷ Add pine nuts and some lemon juice and season with salt and pepper. If raisins are not sweet enough, add some more sugar.

Serves 4

2 tablespoons pine nuts
1 tablespoon capers
1 tablespoon raisins
8 tablespoons olive oil
Some lemon juice
Salt
Freshly ground white pepper

Orange Vinaigrette

This marinade is an ideal basic vinaigrette for dressing salads or marinating fish and poultry. It can be varied endlessly according to taste. One idea: monkfish carpaccio with orange vinaigrette.

❶ Mix orange juice and peel with olive oil and season with honey, salt and pepper.

❷ Add thyme leaves to vinaigrette and let stand for a while.

Serves 4

Juice and peel of 1 organically
   grown orange
5 tablespoons olive oil
1 tablespoon acacia honey
Thyme leaves
Salt
Freshly ground white pepper

Tomato Sauce

It is best to always cook a large amount of tomato sauce. It keeps in the refrigerator for a few days and you can have a delicious meal ready in no time for surprise guests or after a long day at work. A pot of pasta is cooked quickly and with home-made tomato sauce, fresh basil and grated parmesan you have a wonderful meal on the table.

Makes about 3/4 l sauce

2 carrots, peeled

1/2 celery root, peeled

1 parsley root, peeled

2 onions, peeled

4 garlic cloves, unpeeled and pressed

1 tablespoon tomato paste

1 can of peeled tomatoes, 800 g

2 sprigs of thyme

1 sprig of rosemary

1 sprig of sage

2 bay leaves

2 cloves

3 peppercorns

4 stem tomatoes, peeled and seeded

Olive oil

Salt

Sugar

❸ Cut tomatoes into coarse cubes and add to sauce after it has cooked for 20 minutes.

❹ Slowly simmer tomato sauce for about 2 hours. Add water or stock if necessary.

❺ Strain sauce through a sieve and lightly salt and allow to cool completely. Fill in jars with lids and refrigerate.

❶ Cut root vegetables and onions into 1 cm cubes and sauté in a pot with 2 tablespoons olive oil. Sprinkle with 1 level tablespoon sugar, add tomato paste and roast for an additional 5 minutes.

❷ Add herbs and pour in peeled tomatoes. Fill can half full with water, turn to catch remaining tomato juice and pour into pot. Add bay leaf, peppercorns and cloves.

6. Antipasti, Salads and Side Dishes

Sicilian Orange Salad with Fennel and Olives

Any fennel lover will be thrilled by this salad. It is a great side dish with sautéed cod or pike-perch. But it is just as great a treat by itself served with fresh baguette.

Serves 4

3 oranges

2 small red onions

2 small fennel bulbs

100 g black olives (Kalamata)

4 tablespoons olive oil

1 tablespoon white wine vinegar

Salt

Sugar

Freshly ground black pepper

❻ Arrange sliced fennel, orange fillets and olives on plates and drizzle with orange marinade.

❼ Coarsely chop fennel greens, crush pepper corns with mortar and pestle and sprinkle over salad.

Add crayfish or shrimps and this delicious salad is a treat for eyes and palate on any buffet.

❶ Generously cut off orange peel with a sharp knife so all white skin is removed.

❷ Remove orange fillets from skin and catch all the juice.

❸ Mix orange juice with white wine vinegar and olive oil and season with salt, a pinch of sugar and pepper.

❹ Peel onions, cut in half and cut lengthwise into thin segments.

❺ Remove green parts and stalks of fennel. Carefully slice fennel into thin slices with a mandolin or electric slicer. If you have neither kitchen tool, use a sharp knife to cut fennel into very thin slices.

Tramezzini with Scrambled Eggs and Ham

❶ Mix crème fraîche with mustard and season with salt and pepper. Spread onto one side of eight pieces of toast and onto both sides of 4 pieces of toast and set aside.

❷ Break eggs, add milk and stir together thoroughly. Allow to set in hot butter, stirring constantly. After about 1 minute, add ham. Divide one half of the scrambled eggs over 4 slices of toast, cover with the pieces of toast which are buttered on both sides, and place remaining scrambled eggs on top. Top with toast and cut diagonally in half.

2 tablespoons crème fraîche

1 teaspoon hot mustard

Salt

Freshly ground black pepper

12 slices of toast, crust removed

8 eggs, medium size

50 ml milk

1 tablespoon unsalted butter

150 g ham, thinly sliced and cut into 1 cm square pieces

Bruscetta with Lukewarm Octopus

❶ Thoroughly wash octopus. Bring 1 l water, vegetables for making soup, 2 garlic cloves, larded onion and white wine to a boil. Season with salt, a pinch of sugar, fennel seeds and pepper corns and simmer octopus in liquid for about 50 minutes.

❷ In the meantime, rub pieces of bread with halved cloves of garlic and toast in a skillet in hot olive oil on both sides until golden brown. Season in skillet with a pinch of salt and pepper. Drain on paper towel. Preheat oven to 160 °C.

❸ Remove octopus from water, allow to cool slightly and cut into 2 cm pieces. Add 2 tablespoons olive oil, parsley and lemon juice and season with salt and pepper. Heat toasted pieces of bread in preheated oven. Divide octopus salad over toasted bread and garnish with fresh basil leaves.

Serves 4

400g octopus, cleaned and
    kitchen-ready

Vegetables for making soup
    (e.g. carrots, leeks, celery)

4 garlic cloves, peeled

1 larded onion (peeled onion
    larded with 1 bay leaf and
    2 cloves)

l/4 l dry white wine

Salt

A pinch of sugar

Freshly ground black pepper

1/2 teaspoon fennel seeds

5 black pepper corns

16 slices of white bread

Olive oil

1 tablespoon flat-leaf parsley,
chopped

Juice of 1 lemon

A few leaves of basil

Sautéed Veal Tartare with Porcini Mushrooms

2 small onions, peeled

Olive oil

1 sprig of thyme

400 g veal (plate)

Salt

Freshly ground black pepper

Freshly ground nutmeg

1 tablespoon capers

4 anchovies

2 egg yolks, medium size

1 teaspoon Dijon mustard

1 dash of cognac

250 g porcini mushrooms

1 tablespoon flat-leaf parsley, finely chopped

1 tablespoon unsalted butter

❶ Dice onions and sauté in 1 tablespoon olive oil until soft and translucent. Add plucked thyme leaves. Pass veal and cooled onions through meat grinder on coarse setting.

❷ Season meat paste with salt, pepper and nutmeg. Add chopped capers, anchovies, egg yolks, mustard and cognac and mix thoroughly. Clean porcini mushrooms, cut into 1/2 cm thick slices with a knife or a mandolin.

❸ Shape veal into 8 oval patties and sauté in hot olive oil on both sides for about 4 minutes. Sauté porcini mushrooms in a grill pan on both sides and season with salt, pepper and parsley. Toss with butter shortly before serving. Serve sautéed veal tartar with porcini mushrooms and fresh baguette.

Serves 4

Peperonata with Garlic

2 red peppers, halved and seeded

2 yellow peppers, halved and seeded

2 garlic cloves, peeled

3 tablespoons olive oil

1 tablespoon sugar

1 tablespoon paprika powder, sweet

A dash of white wine vinegar

Salt

Cayenne pepper

Peperonata goes well with sautéed fish and meat, but can also be served cold as an antipasto.

❶ Peel peppers with a peeler and cut into very thin strips. Finely chop garlic and sauté in hot olive oil until soft and translucent. Add pepper strips, sprinkle with sugar and lightly caramelise. Dust with paprika powder, add white wine vinegar, cover and cook until paste thickens over low heat. (If necessary add some water or stock). Season with salt and cayenne pepper to taste.

Serves 4

Raw Artichoke Salad with Grated Parmesan Cheese

This edible thistle can be purchased year-round, but artichokes taste best in the spring and fall. Customarily, artichokes are carefully cleaned and cooked immediately afterwards in boiling salted water with lemon juice for about 30 minutes. They taste especially delicious quartered or sliced and sautéed in oil. Artichokes are great appetizers, since they contain cynarin, a bitter substance, which acts as an appetite stimulant.

❶ Peel away the outer hard leaves of the artichokes. Cut off the prickly points of the remaining leaves. Scrape out the fuzzy choke in the centre with a spoon. Immediately place artichokes in cold lemon water (juice of 1 lemon), so they don't turn brown.

❷ Clean arugula, rinse and spin dry. Stir vinegar, a dash of lemon juice and olive oil together and season with salt, pepper and sugar. With a peeler, shave off thin parmesan strips.

❸ Thinly slice artichokes with a knife or mandolin.

❹ Arrange arugula and artichokes on plates, sprinkle with parmesan and drizzle with oil-vinegar marinade. Cut remaining lemon in quarters and serve with artichoke salad. Baguette or rosemary bread goes best with the salad.

Serves 4

8 small artichokes

2 lemons

1 bunch of arugula

1 tablespoon Balsamic vinegar

Juice of 1/2 lemon

6 tablespoons olive oil

Salt

A pinch of sugar

Freshly ground black pepper

Fresh parmesan cheese by the piece

Bagna caôda
Vegetable Fondue with
Hot Anchovy Sauce

4 stalks celery

2 carrots

1 red pepper

1 yellow pepper

1 fennel bulb

1 zucchini

12 anchovies

3 garlic cloves, peeled

1 tablespoon capers

8 tablespoons olive oil

2 tablespoons unsalted butter

1 tablespoon flat-leaf parsley,
   finely chopped

Freshly ground black pepper

Salt

This Piedmontian vegetable fondue serves as a perfect alternative to the traditional meat fondue. The flavourful spiciness of the anchovies adds an interesting touch to the vegetables. Plenty of crisp bread and a cool glass of white wine, preferably Arneis, taste best with bagna cauda.

❶ Wash celery, peel carrots, halve peppers and remove seeds. Halve fennel as well and remove stalk.

❷ Cut celery, carrots, peppers, fennel and zucchini in about 1/2 cm thick and 5 cm long sticks. Until used, wrap vegetables in a damp piece of cloth and chill.

❸ Finely chop anchovies, garlic and capers separately. Heat 4 table-spoons olive oil and sauté garlic until soft and translucent. Add anchovies and simmer for an additional 2 minutes, stirring constantly. Shortly before serving, stir in remaining olive oil, capers and butter and briefly bring to a boil.

❹ Finish hot thick anchovy sauce with finely chopped parsley, black pepper and a pinch of salt and serve with the vegetables.

Serves 4

Insalata Caprese Mozzarella with Tomatoes and Fried Basil

Insalata Caprese – the favourite among popular Italian dishes, is enjoyed and loved all over the world by now. Especially in the summer, ripe tomatoes, fresh basil and the fresh, milky flavour of mozzarella taste delicious.

❶ Remove mozzarella from brine, drain and cut into 1/2 cm thick slices. Wash tomatoes, remove green stem ends and slice as well.

❷ Pluck basil leaves and fry in hot oil. Fry leaves individually, since the liquid of the leaves evaporates when they are cooked and the oil might spatter. Drain basil on paper towel.

❸ There are numerous ways to arrange tomatoes and mozzarella. You can arrange them alternately on top of each other or separately. Season tomato and mozzarella slices with salt and pepper, drizzle with olive oil and Balsamic vinegar and finish with fried basil leaves.

If desired, you can of course use fresh basil leaves as well.

Serves 4

2 packages of mozzarella
   (125 g each)
4 Italian stem tomatoes
1 bunch of fresh basil
Oil for frying
Salt
Coarsely ground black pepper
4 tablespoons olive oil
2 tablespoons Balsamic vinegar

Marinated Vegetables

1 eggplant

1 zucchini

1 red pepper

1 yellow pepper

1 whole garlic, halved

1/2 bunch of flat-leaf parsley

2 sprigs of rosemary

4 sprigs of thyme

1/2 bunch of basil

2 garlic cloves, peeled

Olive oil

Salt

Sugar

Freshly ground black pepper

Takes some work, but the result is well worth it. Vegetables prepared this way are simply irresistible.

❶ Cut eggplant and zucchini into 1 cm thick slices and salt lightly. Preheat oven to 180 °C.

❷ Halve pepper and remove seeds. Place in a skillet with the skin side turned up, add halved garlics, 1 sprig of rosemary and 2 sprigs of thyme and drizzle with 4 tablespoons olive oil. Bake in preheated oven for about 30 minutes.

❸ In the meantime, pat sliced eggplant and zucchini dry with paper towel and sauté in a skillet in hot olive oil on both sides until golden brown. Remove from skillet and drain on paper towel.

❹ Remove peppers from oven, peel off skin and cut into 2 cm thick strips. Remove remaining rosemary and thyme from sprigs and place into a tall glass with plucked basil leaves and individual cloves of garlic. Add 120 ml olive oil and finely purée using a hand blender. Season with salt, pepper and a pinch of sugar.

❺ Brush herb oil onto both sides of eggplant, zucchini and peppers, cover and marinate in the refrigerator for 2 hours. Remove from refrigerator about 20 minutes prior to the meal and serve with baguette.

Serves 4

Sweet-and-Sour Yellow Onions

The sweet-and-sour taste of sugar and vinegar goes well with these tender onions. Onions can be served by themselves as an antipasto or with braised fish. These delicious onions also taste good with grilled swordfish or monkfish as a fancy side dish.

❶ Soak onions in cold water for about 20 minutes – this helps remove the tight peel. Peel onions and simmer in salted water that is just about to boil over low heat for about 20 minutes. Cook sugar with water over low heat until a caramel-coloured syrup forms. Add Balsamic vinegar and drained onions and caramelise while rotating skillet. Shortly before serving, add butter, rotate skillet and lightly season with salt and pepper

Serves 4

16 yellow onions

Salt

4 tablespoons sugar

2 tablespoons water

4 tablespoons Balsamic vinegar

1 tablespoon unsalted butter

Freshly ground black pepper

Caramelised Carrots with Raisins and Mint

Tastes good lukewarm as an antipasto or hot with sautéed meat and poultry dishes.

❶ Cut carrots diagonally into 4 cm slices and boil in plenty of salted-water. Drain carrots in a colander. Lightly caramelise 2 tablespoons of sugar with a few drops of water, add carrots and briefly rotate. Add a dash of mineral water and simmer for an additional 5 minutes.

❷ Add drained raisins to carrots and lightly season with salt and pepper. Sauté diced shallots in butter until soft and translucent and fold into vegetables with torn mint leaves.

4 carrots, peeled

Salt

2 tablespoons sugar

Mineral water

2 tablespoons raisins
(soaked in lukewarm black tea)

Freshly ground black pepper

1 shallot, peeled and diced

2 tablespoons unsalted butter

2 sprigs of mint

**12 slices of Parma ham
(sliced extremely thin)**

4 fresh figs

Olive oil

Freshly ground black pepper

1 package of Grissini

Fresh Figs with Parma Ham and Grissini

No great preparation is needed for figs and Parma ham. The most important thing is purchasing the right ingredients. Only truly ripe and flavourful figs and top-quality Parma ham that is sliced extremely thin should be purchased. Figs and Parma ham can be served by themselves as a snack with a glass of red wine or as an appetizer to an Italian dinner.

❶ Divide Parma ham into portions and arrange on plates.

❷ Cut an x in the top of the figs, press them flat and divide over plates.

❸ Drizzle Parma ham with olive oil and sprinkle with coarse pepper.

❹ Serve Grissini with Parma ham and if desired sprinkle with freshly grated parmesan cheese.

As an appetizer, roll Parma ham around Grissini sticks and arrange on an oval platter. Cut figs into small pieces and use as garnish for platter.

Serves 4

Panzanella
Bread Salad

A quick and tasty use for left-overs. One starts out with stale bread – all the other ingredients are up to you and your imagination. Marinated bread is flaked into pieces and combined with ham, diced cucumbers, tomatoes, zucchini, peppers, or onions – it all depends upon season and taste. Panzanella can serve as a small meal, a great appetizer or a tasty snack.

❶ Flake olive bread into bite-sized pieces. Cut tomatoes into thin strips and onions into extremely thin slices.

❷ Coarsely chop anchovies and onions. Peel eggs and quarter with a knife or an egg cutter. Thinly slice celery diagonally.

❸ Mix all ingredients in a mixing bowl. Add capers and parsley. Blend lemon juice, olive oil and white wine vinegar together, pour over panzanella and toss with a salad serving set. Season with salt, pepper and a pinch of sugar.

❹ Tear flavourful leaves of celery into small pieces and sprinkle over panzanella.

Serves 4

250 g olive bread or ciabatta
  bread
2 tomatoes, peeled and seeded
2 small red onions, peeled
12 anchovies
80 g black olives, pitted
3 hard-boiled eggs
2 stalks celery with leaves
2 tablespoons capers
3 sprigs flat-leaf parsley,
  torn into pieces
Juice of 1 lemon
8 tablespoons olive oil
2 tablespoons white wine
  vinegar
Salt
A pinch of sugar
Freshly ground black pepper

Vitello tonnato
Cold Veal with Tuna-Caper Sauce

700 g veal (tail piece)

Salt

Freshly ground white pepper

2 sprigs of thyme

2 garlic cloves, unpeeled
   and pressed

2 tablespoons olive oil

6 anchovies

1 1/2 tablespoons capers,
   chopped

2 shallots, peeled and diced

2 cans of tuna in oil

4 tablespoons mayonnaise

50 g liquid sweet cream

50 ml dry white wine

1 tablespoon chopped parsley

1 lemon for garnishing

Sugar

This favourite summer dish brings back beautiful vacation memories. It tastes best on a balcony with a glass of cool fruity white wine.

❶ Preheat oven to 190 °C. Season veal with salt and pepper and slightly sauté in 1 tablespoon olive oil on both sides. Add thyme and garlic and bake in preheated oven for about 45 minutes. From time to time pour some water over meat.

❷ Sauté anchovies, capers and onions in remaining olive oil until soft and translucent, season with salt and pepper and allow to cool. Mix tuna pieces, mayonnaise, cream, white wine and cooled onion mixture together and finely purée with a hand blender. Season with salt, pepper and a pinch of sugar. Finish with parsley.

❸ Cut cooled veal into very thin slices and arrange in a circle on plates. Brush with tuna sauce and serve with lemon wedges.

Veal and sauce keep well in refrigerator for 2-3 days separately. So you magically have a delicious dinner ready at any time.

Serves 4

7. Soups and Stews

Zuppa di Pomodori Tomato Soup with Pesto and Garlic Croûtons

500 g ripe tomatoes

2 onions, peeled

4 garlic cloves, peeled

1 carrot, peeled

3 stalks celery

1 parsley root

2 sprigs of thyme

1 tablespoon tomato paste

1 can peeled tomatoes (800 g)

1/2 l stock

Salt

A pinch of sugar

Freshly ground black pepper

Cayenne pepper

6 pieces of toast

Olive oil

2 tablespoons unsalted butter

2 tablespoons pesto

(see page 29)

Who can resist a freshly prepared tomato soup? It tastes even better if you sprinkle freshly grated parmesan or Pecorino cheese over the hot soup. A hot tip for summer: serve soup chilled. It tastes refreshing and fills you at the same time.

❶ Remove green stem end of tomatoes and cut into coarse cubes. Finely dice onions and 2 cloves of garlic. Cut carrots, celery and parsley root into pieces.

❷ Sauté onions and 3 cloves of garlic in 3 tablespoons olive oil until soft and translucent. Add carrots, celery, parsley root, thyme and tomato paste and cook for an additional 5 minutes, stirring occasionally.

❸ Add peeled tomatoes and stock and simmer over low heat for about 45 minutes. Season with salt, sugar, pepper and cayenne pepper to taste.

❹ In the meantime, prepare bread croûtons. Cut toast into 2 cm cubes. Thinly slice remaining garlic. Heat butter in skillet and slowly sauté bread cubes on all sides until golden brown. Add garlic and sauté with croûtons. Season with salt and pepper and drain on paper towel. Keep warm in preheated oven.

❺ Strain tomato soup through a sieve, ladle into deep plates, add bread croutons and drizzle with some pesto.

Serves 4

Savoy Cabbage Stew with Fontina Cheese and Sage

120 g chick peas

600 g Savoy cabbage

2 onions

3 tablespoons olive oil

1 l vegetable broth

1 bay leaf

1/2 bunch of parsley

3 sage leaves, finely chopped

Salt

Freshly ground white pepper

Freshly ground nutmeg

12 small pieces of farmers' bread

180 g grated Fontina cheese

This mild and tasty cheese from the Aosta valley is made from cows' milk. Its creamy consistency makes this cheese very suitable for cooking.

❶ Soak chickpeas in plenty of water, preferably overnight. Clean Savoy cabbage, remove stalk and cut into bite-sized pieces.

❷ Peel onions, halve and cut into small strips. Sauté onions and chopped Savoy cabbage briefly in olive oil, add drained chick peas and pour in vegetable broth. Add bay leaf and simmer slowly for about 45 minutes.

❸ The stew tastes best if chickpeas are very soft. Before serving, fold in coarsely chopped parsley and sage leaves and season with salt, pepper and freshly ground nutmeg. Preheat oven to 200 °C.

❹ Sprinkle slices of bread with cheese and bake in preheated oven under high heat from above until golden brown.

❺ Ladle soup into deep plates and serve with bread slices.

Serves 4

Chickpea Soup with Pancetta

Pancetta is unsmoked, streaky bacon. It is rubbed with salt, herbs and spices, rolled up and dried. Pancetta can be served raw and cut into extremely thin slices as an antipasto. When it is sautéed, pancetta adds a delicious, flavourful taste to any dish.

❶ Drain chick peas in a colander and rinse under cold water. Finely dice carrots, onions and celery and steam in hot olive oil for about 5 minutes.

❷ Add chickpeas and thyme. Pour in beef stock and simmer uncovered over low heat for about 30 minutes.

❸ Cut Pancetta into 1/2 cm strips and sauté in a skillet until crisp. Coarsely purée stew using a hand blender and season with salt, pepper and freshly ground nutmeg. Ladle stew into deep plates and sprinkle with crisp Pancetta.

Serves 4

1 small can chickpeas

1 carrot, peeled

1 onion, peeled

1/4 celery root

3/4 l vegetable stock

2 sprigs of thyme

80 g Pancetta in one piece

2 tablespoons olive oil

Salt

Freshly ground black pepper

Freshly ground nutmeg

Zuppa di pesce
Fish Soup with White Wine, Tomatoes and Fresh Basil

The ingredients for the fish soup depend upon the selection at the market. Best are white-flesh fishes, mussels and prawns. Whole prawns and mussels add a very intense flavour to the soup.

❶ Water mussels in plenty of water for about 2 hours. Keep changing the water. Then rinse and clean mussels. Cut monkfish fillet into 2 cm pieces.

❷ In the meantime, finely dice onions, garlic, celery, fennel (stalk removed) and tomatoes.

❸ Briefly sauté celery and fennel in 1 tablespoon olive oil, add a dash of white wine and pour in fish stock. Simmer for about 15 minutes over low heat and season with salt, pepper and cayenne pepper to taste.

❹ Sauté onions and garlic in remaining olive oil until soft and translucent, add mussels and cover. Allow mussels to open, moving the pot from time to time. Add remaining white wine, pour in vegetable-tomato-broth and simmer over low heat for about 5 minutes. Season monkfish with salt and pepper and add to soup with gamberini. Remove soup from stove and let stand for 5 minutes.

❺ Season fish soup with a few saffron threads, salt and cayenne pepper, finish with finely chopped basil and serve with fresh baguette.

Serves 4

400 g vongole
400 g blue mussels
120 g monkfish fillets
1 onion, peeled
2 garlic cloves, peeled
2 stalks celery
1 fennel bulb, cleaned
2 tomatoes, peeled and seeded
2 tablespoons olive oil
1/4 l dry white wine
1/2 l fish stock
Salt
Cayenne pepper
Freshly ground black pepper
8 raw gamberini, with head
1/2 bunch of basil
Some threads of saffron

Livornese Dried Cod Stew with Tomatoes and Caper Oil

400 g dried cod (middle piece)

1/2 l milk

1 larded onion (peeled onion
    larded with 1 bay leaf and
    2 cloves)

500 g tomatoes, peeled and
seeded

1 carrot, peeled

1 parsley root, peeled

2 potatoes, peeled

2 stalks celery

1 shallot, peeled

2 garlic cloves, peeled

6 tablespoons olive oil

1/2 l fish stock

1 sprig of thyme

1 sprig of basil

2 tablespoons capers

Salt

Freshly ground black pepper

Cayenne pepper

In Mediterranean countries, dried cod dishes are very popular. What used to be an important way to preserve fresh cod is now a delicacy that you should try at least once.

❶ Pound dried cod lightly with a meat pounder. Bring equal amounts of milk and water to a boil, add larded onion and remove from stove. Soak dried cod in the liquid for about 2 1/2 hours, turning fish from time to time.

❷ Finely dice tomatoes, carrot, celery, parsley root, potatoes, shallots and garlic. Heat 2 tablespoons olive oil and sauté vegetables (without tomatoes) for about 5 minutes until soft and translucent. Do not allow vegetables to brown. Add tomatoes, pour in fish stock and simmer for 20 minutes.

❸ Remove dried cod, drain well and remove skin and any brown parts. Cut into 5 cm pieces, add to soup and simmer for another 10 minutes.

❹ Finely chop thyme, basil and capers and mix with remaining olive oil. Season soup with salt, pepper and cayenne pepper to taste. Serve soup in deep plates and drizzle with caper oil.

Serves 4

Cream of Rice Soup with Green Beans

❶ Briefly sauté diced shallots in butter, then add rice and pour in white wine. Add stock and simmer for about 20 minutes until rice is very tender. Add cream and purée with a hand blender. Strain through a sieve.

❷ Clean beans, cut diagonally into 3 cm pieces and cook in plenty of salted water until soft. Add to cream of rice soup and season with salt, white pepper and freshly ground nutmeg.

❸ Before serving, add small pieces of summer savory to soup and arrange in deep plates.

Serves 4

2 shallots, diced

2 tablespoons unsalted butter

150 g round grain rice

60 ml dry white wine

600 ml vegetables stock

150 g cream

200 g green beans

Salt

Freshly ground white pepper

1 sprig of summer savory

Minestrone with Pasta

❶ Finely dice onions, garlic, fennel (stalk removed), zucchini and tomatoes. Heat olive oil and sauté onions and garlic until soft and translucent. Add carrots and fennel, pour in stock and simmer slowly for 30 minutes. After 15 minutes, add remaining vegetables and tomatoes.

❷ Cook risoni in boiling salted water for 10 minutes, drain and add to soup. Season minestrone with salt and pepper. If desired, finish with cayenne pepper and basil. Serve sprinkled with freshly grated parmesan cheese.

Serves 4

1 onion, peeled

1 clove garlic, peeled

2 carrots, peeled

1 fennel bulb, cleaned

1 zucchini

2 tomatoes, peeled and seeded

2 tablespoons olive oil

3/4 l stock

60 g risoni (rice-shaped pasta)

Salt

Freshly ground black pepper

Cayenne pepper

Basil leaves, finely chopped

Freshly grated parmesan cheese

8. Pasta, Ravioli and Gnocchi

Capellini aglio e olio
Capellini with Garlic and Olive Oil

2 garlic cloves, peeled

2 peperoncini, dried

500 g capellini

Salt

6 tablespoons olive oil

Freshly ground black pepper

2 tablespoons unsalted butter

One of the basic rules for cooking Italian pasta: always keep some of the pasta water for the sauce. The water contains starch which helps bind the sauce and intensify the flavour.

❶ Thinly slice garlic. Crush peperoncini with mortar and pestle or chop with a knife. The seeds of these small pods are very hot. If you do not like your food too spicy, halve peperoncini and remove seeds before chopping.

❷ Cook capellini in plenty of boiling salted water for 3 minutes.

❸ In the meantime, heat olive oil, sauté garlic and add peperoncini.

❹ Drain pasta in a colander, catching the pasta water in a dish. Add hot pasta to olive oil and pour one ladle of pasta water over pasta. Season with salt and pepper and finish with butter.

❺ Depending on taste, sprinkle with fresh herbs, e.g. chopped parsley or fresh basil, and serve immediately.

Serves 4

Cannelloni with Melted Tomatoes and Cheese Sauce

Dough rolls can be filled with whatever your heart desires e.g. a hearty meat stuffing or a vegetarian artichoke-potato stuffing. You can purchase ready-made cannelloni and fill them with any fancy stuffing, but there is nothing as delicious as home-made cannelloni.

Serves 4

For 20 pasta sheets 10 cm x 10 cm

500 g leg of turkey, bones removed

Salt

2 tablespoons oil

Freshly ground black pepper

1 carrot, peeled

1 stalk celery

1 onion, peeled

2 garlic cloves, peeled

1 sprig of thyme

1 sprig of rosemary

1/2 bunch of flat-leaf parsley

3 tablespoons unsalted butter

2 tablespoons flour

200 ml milk

100 g cream

2 tomatoes, peeled, seeded and diced

80 g grated Bel Paese cheese

❹ Heat 2 tablespoons butter until foamy. Stir in flour and add milk and cream, one tablespoon at a time. Simmer béchamel sauce over low heat for about 10 minutes, stirring occasionally. Season with salt and pepper and pass through a fine-mesh sieve.

❺ Grease oven-proof dish with remaining butter. Evenly place cannelloni into dish and pour béchamel sauce over the cannelloni.

❻ Sprinkle with diced tomatoes and cheese and bake in preheated oven for about 25 minutes until golden brown. If desired, drizzle with herb oil or pesto.

❶ Season leg of turkey with salt and pepper and sauté in a casserole dish in heated olive oil on both sides. Preheat oven to 180 °C. Coarsely chop carrots, celery and onion and add to meat with garlic. Bake uncovered in preheated oven for about 1 1/2 hours. After 30 minutes of baking, add 1/8 l water and baste leg of turkey with liquid from time to time.

❷ Remove leg of turkey from oven and allow to cool completely. Cut into 1 cm slices and pass with vegetables through fine setting of meat grinder. Season with salt and pepper and finish with finely chopped parsley.

❸ Spread out freshly prepared pasta sheets, stuff with meat paste and roll up. If you are using purchased cannelloni, fill tubes with mixture.

Lasagne with Meat Sauce and Mozzarella

25 g unsalted butter

30 g flour

1/2 l milk

1 bay leaf

1 sprig of thyme

2 crushed pepper corns

Salt

Freshly ground nutmeg.

600 g mixed chopped meat

2 tablespoons olive oil

1 onion, peeled

2 garlic cloves, peeled

1 tablespoon tomato paste

1 can peeled tomatoes (800 g)

Cayenne pepper

Freshly ground black pepper

A pinch of oregano, dried

Butter for greasing baking dish

250 g sheets of lasagne
   (16 sheets)

100 g grated Edam cheese

1 ball of mozzarella (125 g)

The smell of melted cheese, pasta and meat sauce alone will lure all your hungry guests, children and adults, into the kitchen.

❶ Heat butter and slowly add flour while whisking. Keep whisking until a smooth mixture forms. Set flour mixture aside. Bring milk to a boil, add herbs and spices and let sit for 10 minutes.

❷ Pass milk through a sieve and slowly pour into flour mixture while whisking. Heat and boil for 15 minutes, stirring constantly. Pass through sieve and lightly season with salt and nutmeg.

❸ Season chopped meat with salt and pepper and sauté in a skillet with 2 tablespoons olive oil until crumbly. Add finely chopped onions, garlic and tomato paste and sauté for another 5 minutes. Pour in crushed peeled tomatoes and simmer slowly for about 25 minutes while stirring from time to time. Season with salt, pepper, cayenne pepper and a pinch of oregano. Preheat oven to 180 °C.

❹ Butter a rectangular baking dish. Starting with the lasagne sheets, layer béchamel sauce, meat sauce, grated Edam cheese and lasagne sheets into dish. Finish with meat sauce. Top with sliced mozzarella cheese and bake in preheated oven for 35 minutes.

Serves 4

Cannelloni Stuffed with Walnuts, Robiola and Poultry Liver

In addition, you can add sautéed apple or pear pieces to the walnut stuffing. In that case, pour some Calvados over poultry liver.

❶ Lightly roast grated walnuts in 1 tablespoon hot butter and allow to cool. Cut poultry liver into small cubes and slowly sauté in 1 tablespoon hot butter. Season lightly with salt and pepper. Fold walnuts, cooled liver and egg yolks into Italian cream cheese. Season with salt, white pepper and nutmeg. Preheat oven to 180 °C.

❷ Roll out dough into an extremely thin sheet and spread mixture on top. Roll up into cannelloni as thick as a finger. Layer into buttered casserole dish and pour cream on top. Bake in preheated oven for about 20 minutes.

❸ Thinly slice artichokes and sauté in olive oil over low heat with garlic and sprigs of thyme. Season with salt and pepper.

❹ Arrange individual portions of canneloni and sautéed artichokes on flat plates.

Serves 4

For 20 sheets of pasta dough
  10 x 10 cm
  (see recipe on page 22)
120 g grated walnuts
3 tablespoons unsalted butter
350 g poultry liver
2 egg yolks
300 g robiola
  (Italian cream cheese)
Salt
Freshly ground white pepper
Freshly ground nutmeg
120 g cream
4 cleaned artichoke hearts
2 tablespoons olive oil
1 clove garlic, unpeeled and
  pressed
2 sprigs of thyme

Bevette all'amatriciana Pasta with Onion Sauce and Chopped Egg

3 white onions, peeled

2 garlic cloves, peeled

200 g streaky bacon,
  rind removed

4 tomatoes

2 tablespoons olive oil

1 can peeled tomatoes in
  pieces (400 g)

Salt

Freshly ground black pepper

1 tablespoon flat-leaf parsley,
  chopped

2 hard-boiled eggs

Parmesan cheese

The selection of the different pasta types is very important. For strong and sturdy pasta, e.g. bevette and linguine, strong sauces are suitable. The sauce clings easily to the pasta and if you like sauces, it tastes delicious.

❶ Halve onions and cut into strips. Finely chop garlic. Cut bacon into 1/2 cm thick strips.

❷ Remove green stem end of tomatoes, cut an x in the top and blanch in boiling water for 2 minutes. Remove with skimmer, rinse under ice cold water and peel off skin. Cut into quarters, take out seeds and cut into strips as well.

❸ Sauté onions and bacon in 2 tablespoons olive oil and add canned tomato pieces. Simmer onion sauce slowly for about 15 minutes, add tomato strips and season with salt and pepper.

❹ Cook bevette until al dente, following directions on package, and drain in a colander, catching some of the pasta water in a dish.

❻ Toss pasta with onion sauce, adding a small ladle of pasta water, and finish with chopped parsley. Arrange pasta on plates and sprinkle with chopped egg.

Serves 4

Orecchiette with Broccoli and Red Onions

This pasta is named after the word "l'orecchia – ear". To make "ear" pasta prepare a dough with semolina, flour, water and olive oil, cut into thin slices and form little ears. But you can purchase good quality orecchiette in stores as well.

❶ Remove leaves and coarse stalk from broccoli. Peel stalk and cut into small pieces. Depending upon size, halve broccoli flowerets or cut into quarters. Cook in plenty of salted water until al dente, drain in a colander and rinse under ice cold water.

❷ Half red onions and cut into strips. Remove stalk of dandelion and flake into bite-sized pieces. Thoroughly wash and spin dry.

❸ Cook orecchiette in plenty of salted water for 12 minutes and drain in a colander, catching the pasta water in a dish.

❹ In the meantime, sauté onions in 2 tablespoons olive oil until soft and translucent, add broccoli and garlic and slowly sauté for an additional 5 minutes. Add dandelion and orecchiette and pour a few tablespoons pasta water over it. Add remaining olive oil and butter, quickly rotate and season with salt, peperoncino and black pepper to taste. It desired, finish with chopped anchovies and freshly grated parmesan cheese.

Serves 4

600 g broccoli

2 red onions

1 head of Italian dandelion

500 g orecchiette

Salt

4 tablespoons olive oil

2 garlic cloves, peeled

2 tablespoons unsalted butter

A pinch of peperoncino, dried

Freshly ground black pepper

Linguine with Diced Eggplant

400 g eggplants

Salt

500 g tomatoes, peeled and seeded

2 tablespoons olive oil

2 onions, peeled and diced

1 clove garlic, peeled and finely chopped

1 sprig of rosemary

A pinch of sugar

1 tablespoon tomato paste

1/4 l vegetable stock

500 g linguine

Freshly ground white pepper

2 chili peppers, finely diced

1 sprig of basil

1 tablespoon unsalted butter

Of course, this Southern Italian dish tastes best if prepared with sun-ripened, flavourful eggplants.

❶ Wash eggplant, remove stem end, cut into 1/2 cm cubes and salt lightly. Set aside for 10 minutes and dry with kitchen paper. Finely dice tomatoes.

❷ Heat olive oil in a skillet and sauté onion, garlic and diced eggplant until soft and translucent. Add rosemary, a pinch of sugar and tomato paste and sauté over low heat for an additional 2 minutes. Pour in vegetable stock and slowly simmer for 10 minutes.

❸ In the meantime, cook linguine al dente in plenty of salted water for 8-10 minutes. Drain in a colander. Remove rosemary sprig from sauce, add diced tomatoes and butter and season with salt, pepper and chili peppers to taste. Mix with hot linguine and torn basil leaves and serve immediately.

Serves 4

Ravioli with Sage Butter

If you have the necessary time it is well worth it to prepare home-made ravioli for a change. You will notice the difference at the latest at your first bite. It is a good idea to prepare a larger amount. Freeze additional ravioli separately on a baking sheet, afterwards fill individual portions into bags. When needed, place frozen ravioli into boiling salted water.

❶ Prepare pasta dough following the recipe for basic pasta dough on page xx, wrap in clingfilm and chill. Preheat oven to 180 °C.

❷ Heat oil in roasting pan. Season pork shoulder with salt and pepper and sauté on both sides. Cut carrots, celery and onions into coarse cubes, lightly press unpeeled garlic and add everything to meat with fresh herbs. Braise uncovered in preheated oven for about 2 1/2 hours. After about 30 minutes, add a cup of water and keep basting pork shoulder with meat juices from time to time.

❸ Remove pork shoulder from oven and allow to cool completely. Cut into strips as thick as a finger, mix with vegetables and pass through fine setting of meat grinder. Season with salt and pepper and finish with finely chopped parsley.

❹ Prepare ravioli following the recipe on page xx.

❺ Place ravioli in boiling salted water, wait for them to rise to the top, remove from heat and let stand for about 2 minutes.

❻ In the meantime, heat butter, add sage leaves flaked into small pieces, rotate and season with salt and pepper. Using a skimmer, carefully take out ravioli from water, drip-dry and arrange on plates, then pour sage butter on top.

Serves 4

Basic recipe for pasta dough
  (see pages 22)

For ravioli filling:
800 g pork shoulder,
  bones removed
Salt
Freshly ground black pepper
3 tablespoons oil
2 carrots, peeled
2 stalks celery
3 onions, peeled
3 garlic cloves
2 sprigs of thyme
2 sprigs of rosemary
1 bunch of flat-leaf parsley

For sage butter:
60 g unsalted butter
3 sprigs of sage

Spaghetti Bolognese

2 stalks celery

1 carrot

2 onions

3 garlic cloves

600 g mixed chopped meat

Salt

Freshly ground black pepper

3 tablespoons olive oil

2 tablespoons tomato paste

1 can peeled tomatoes (800 g)

1 sprig of rosemary

1 sprig of thyme

500 g spaghetti

2 tablespoons unsalted butter

1/2 teaspoon dried oregano

Cayenne pepper

This classic Italian dish is not only loved by children. Add freshly grated parmesan cheese and a few leaves of fresh basil and this traditionally simple dish turns into a special treat.

❶ Wash and clean celery and carrots, peel onions and garlic and finely dice everything. Season chopped meat with salt and pepper and sauté in hot olive oil until crumbly. Add diced vegetables, onions, garlic and tomato paste and sauté for 5 minutes as well. Keep stirring from time to time.

❷ Drain tomatoes in a colander, catching the juice in a dish. Coarsely chop tomatoes and add to chopped meat with juice and fresh herbs. Cover and simmer over low heat for about 1 hour. Keep stirring from time to time.

❸ Bring salted water to a boil and cook spaghetti until al dente for about 8 minutes. Drain in a strainer and allow to drip-dry. Heat butter in a broad pot, add spaghetti, toss and salt lightly.

❹ Season sauce with oregano, salt, pepper and cayenne pepper and serve with spaghetti. Help yourself to freshly grated parmesan as desired.

Serves 4

Pizza with Seafood and Fresh Arugula

500 g flour

1 package of dried yeast

Salt

8 tablespoons olive oil

300 ml water

1 onion, peeled

1 clove garlic, peeled

1 can of peeled tomatoes,
  in pieces (400 g)

1/2 teaspoon dried oregano

Freshly ground black pepper

4 plum tomatoes

2 pieces of mozzarella
  (125 g each)

15 anchovies from jar

16 pieces of cooked shrimps,
  shelled

1 bunch of arugula

The best pizza is made in a traditional wood-fired oven, of course. Yet, in modern households pizza and bread stones serve as a good and sophisticated alternative. Bottom and crust of the pizza turn very crisp and home-made pizza tastes as good as the pizza served at the Italian restaurant around the corner.

❶ Knead flour, yeast, a pinch of salt, 7 tablespoons olive oil and water into a smooth dough. Cover and allow to rest in a warm place.

❷ Finely dice onions and garlic and sauté in 1 tablespoon hot olive oil until soft and translucent. Add tomato pieces and cook into a thick sauce. Season tomato sauce with oregano, salt and pepper.

❸ Separate yeast dough into 4 even pieces and roll out thinly on a floured surface using a rolling pin. Fold in the edges and tightly press together. Preheat oven to 200 °C.

❹ Spread small amount of tomato sauce onto dough. Remove stem end of tomatoes. Thinly slice tomatoes and mozzarella and place on pizzas.

❺ Bake pizzas in preheated oven on pizza stone or baking sheet for about 15 minutes. Wash arugula and flake into pieces. Remove pizzas from oven and top with anchovies, shrimps and arugula. Serve immediately.

Depending on taste, pizza can also be topped with shelled mussels, boiled artichokes and olives. There are no limits on your imagination.

Serves 4-6

Green Maltagliate with Wild Boar Ragoût and Porcini Mushrooms

❶ Prepare green pasta dough following recipe on page 22, wrap in clingfilm and chill.

❷ Remove tendons from wild boar shoulder and cut into coarse cubes. Season meat pieces with salt and pepper and briefly sauté in roasting pan with 2 tablespoons olive oil. Cut carrots, celery and onions into coarse cubes, add to meat and sauté with tomato paste for an additional 5 minutes. Preheat oven to 180 °C.

❸ Coarsely crush spices with mortar and pestle and season meat. Add a dash of red wine and allow some of the liquid to evaporate. Repeat procedure a second time. This adds a beautiful shine to the sauce. Pour in 1/2 l water, cover and slowly braise in preheated oven for about 2 1/2 hours, stirring from time to time. After about one hour pour in remaining water.

❹ Remove meat pieces with a fork and strain sauce through a fine mesh sieve. Depending upon consistency of sauce, allow to thicken some more and season with salt and pepper. Flake meat into small pieces with a fork and add to sauce.

❺ Briefly knead pasta dough, then roll out thinly on floured surface. Using a knife, lengthwise cut out 2 cm wide strips. Cut strips into 3 cm diamond shapes. Bring salted water to a boil and cook maltagliate al dente for about 3 minutes. Drain in a colander and drip-dry.

❻ In the meantime, briefly sauté porcini mushrooms in hot butter on both sides. Add shallots, rotate, season with salt and pepper and finish with parsley. Arrange maltagliate on plates with ragoût and porcini mushrooms.

Serves 4

Green pasta dough
   (see recipe on page 22)
400 g wild boar shoulder
Salt
Freshly ground black pepper
2 tablespoons oil
1 carrot, peeled
1/4 celery root, peeled
4 onions, peeled
2 tablespoons tomato paste
5 pepper corns
2 pimento corns
5 juniper berries
2 cloves
1 bay leaf
1/4 l red wine
3/4 l water
4 porcini mushrooms, cleaned ^
   and sliced (not too thinly)
2 tablespoons unsalted butter
1 shallot, peeled and diced
1 tablespoon parsley, finely
chopped

Spinach-Feta-Dumplings with Sage-Parma-Ham-Butter

500 g fresh spinach

Salt

100 g feta cheese

2 eggs

Freshly ground nutmeg

Freshly ground black pepper

80 g grated baguette

80 g grated parmesan cheese

100 g plain flour

50 g unsalted butter

4 extremely thin slices of
   Parma ham

1 sprig of sage

❶ Rinse and clean spinach and blanch in plenty of salted water. Drain in a colander and rinse under ice cold water. Drip-dry, squeeze dry with hands and chop coarsely.

❷ Mix feta cheese with spinach and eggs, and adjust seasoning with salt, pepper and nutmeg. Carefully work in grated baguette, parmesan cheese and flour until a homogeneous dough forms.

❸ Using 2 teaspoons, cut out small dumplings and place in simmering salted water for 4 minutes.

❹ Heat butter and briefly sauté strips of Parma ham and plucked sage leaves. Carefully remove dumplings with a skimmer, arrange on plates and pour hot butter over dumplings.

Serves 4

Gnocchi with Radicchio, Capers and Olives

❶ Press still warm potatoes through potato ricer onto a floured surface. Heat radicchio in hot butter and sauté until all liquid has evaporated. Allow to cool lightly, then add to potatoes.

❷ Add flour, semolina, egg yolks and salt and knead into a homogeneous dough. Add some more flour if necessary, depending on quality of potatoes.

❸ Roll dough into 2 ropes as thick as a finger. Cut rolls into 2 cm pieces and shape gnocchi using a fork. Drop into plenty of boiling salted water and let them stand for 5 minutes.

❹ Mix pitted olives, capers and garlic with olive oil and season with salt and pepper. Carefully remove gnocchi from cooking water using a skimmer and mix with oil sauce. Serve immediately.

Serves 4

800 g mealy potatoes, boiled and peeled
1 tablespoon unsalted butter
200 g radicchio di Treviso (redleaf lettuce), finely chopped
150 g plain flour
100 g semolina
2 egg yolks
Salt
50 g pitted black olives
1 tablespoon capers
1 pinch of garlic, finely chopped
6 tablespoons olive oil
Freshly ground black pepper

Spaghetti with Prawns, Cucumber and Peperoncini

1 cucumber, peeled

2 garlic cloves, finely chopped

2 dried peperoncini,
   finely crushed

4 tablespoons of olive oil

1 red onion, peeled

500 g spaghetti

Salt

20 pieces of shrimps,
   heads removed and peeled

80 g black olives

2 tablespoons unsalted butter

1 teaspoon flat-leaf parsley,
   finely chopped

❶ Cut cucumber in half lengthwise and into 4 cm long and 1 cm thick sticks. Sauté garlic and peperoncino in olive oil, add cucumbers and prawns and sauté for an additional 4 minutes.

❷ Cut red onions into extremely thin slices or grate. Cook spaghetti in plenty of boiling salted water until al dente for about 8 minutes. Drain in a colander and add to prawns.

❸ Fold into red onions and olives and finish with butter and chopped parsley.

Serves 4

Pappardelle with Pepper Sauce

Red, green and yellow pepper,
   1 each

3 tablespoons olive oil

1 clove garlic, finely chopped

1 tablespoon white wine vinegar

100 ml tomato sauce

Salt

A pinch of sugar

Freshly ground black pepper

30 g unsalted butter

1 small piece of lemon peel from
   organically grown lemon

1 sprig of parsley

1 sprig of oregano

A pinch of caraway seeds

500 g pappardelle
   (broad, long pasta)

❶ Wash peppers, remove seeds and dice. Sauté briefly in olive oil, add garlic, then white wine vinegar. Pour in tomato sauce and simmer over low heat for about 20 minutes. Season with salt, pepper and a pinch of sugar.

❷ Finely chop butter, lemon peel, parsley, oregano, garlic and caraway together.

❸ Cook pappardelle in boiling salted water until al dente. Drain in a colander and immediately mix with pepper sauce. Briefly heat butter mixture, pour over pasta and serve with fresh baguette.

Serves 4

Pumpkin Gnocchi with Salsiccia and Fennel Seeds

If you cannot get salsiccia, you can use lamb sausages or other coarse sausages. It is best to pre-order salsiccia from your local butcher.

❶ Preheat oven to 190 °C. Cut pumpkin into about 4 cm thick wedges. Season with salt, pepper and sugar and wrap in aluminium foil. Slowly bake in preheated oven for about 1 1/2 hours. Unwrap, remove seeds and slowly dry soft flesh in a pot over low heat. Allow pumpkin mousse to cool completely.

❷ Work pumpkin mousse, eggs and flour into a firm dough and shape into small balls. Shape into gnocchi over the back of a fork or with a special gnocchi maker. Until further use, dust with flour and cover with kitchen towel.

❸ Cut salsiccia into 1 cm pieces and sauté in olive oil until golden brown. Season with salt, pepper and fennel seeds.

❹ Simmer pumpkin gnocchi in plenty of salted water for about 5 minutes. Drain in a colander, drip-dry and mix with salsiccia pieces. Finish with butter flakes, toss briefly and serve immediately.

Serves 4

1 kg ripe pumpkin
Salt
Freshly ground white pepper
A pinch of sugar
2 eggs
300 g plain flour
400 g salsiccia
   (raw, coarse Italian sausages)
1 tablespoon olive oil
Freshly ground nutmeg
1/2 teaspoon fennel seeds
1 tablespoon unsalted butter

Spaghetti Aurora Spaghetti with Cream of Tomato Sauce

As with most dishes, the ingredients are the most important factor in this recipe. Only tomatoes with an intense flavour and herbs turn this fairly simple dish into an event. If you like, you can vary the tomato sauce with ham and young peas.

❶ Briefly sauté diced onions and garlic in olive oil. Add diced tomatoes and season with salt, pepper, sugar and a pinch of peperoncino. Simmer until all liquid has evaporated.

❷ Add cream and bring to a boil. Adjust seasoning again and finish with finely chopped basil.

❸ In the meantime, cook spaghetti in plenty of boiling salted water until al dente for about 8 minutes. Drain in a colander and add to tomato sauce.

❹ Toss and arrange on heated deep plates. Serve with freshly grated parmesan cheese – let your guests help themselves.

Serves 4

1 onion, peeled and diced
1 clove garlic, peeled and diced
2 tablespoon olive oil
4 tomatoes, peeled and seeded
Salt
A pinch of sugar
Freshly ground white pepper
Peperoncino
200 g cream
1/2 bunch of basil
500 g spaghetti
50 g freshly grated parmesan
  cheese

Bucatini alla Carbonara

An easy way to feed hungry mouths. This pasta is prepared in no time and promises to be a great success with young and old.

❶ Remove gristle and rind of bacon and cut into small cubes. Peel and dice onions.

❷ Cook bucatini in plenty of boiling salted water until al dente for about 8 minutes. Drain in a colander and drip-dry.

❸ In the meantime, sauté diced bacon and onions in olive oil in a large skillet over low heat until soft and translucent for about 4 minutes.

❹ Stir cream, egg yolks and 30 g parmesan cheese together and season with salt and pepper.

❺ Mix hot pasta with bacon and onions and cover with cream sauce. Briefly heat, stirring from time to time. Do not allow sauce to boil, otherwise egg yolks will set and lose their ability to bind the sauce. If necessary, adjust seasoning of pasta once more and serve immediately. Sprinkle with remaining parmesan cheese at the table if desired.

Serves 4

100 g bacon in 1 piece
1 onion
500 g bucatini
Salt
2 tablespoons olive oil
300 g cream
6 egg yolks
60 g parmesan cheese
Freshly ground black pepper

9. Crespelle, Risotti and Polenta

Crespelle Filled with Spinach and Tomatoes

❶ For the pancake dough, mix flour, milk, butter, whole eggs and 1 egg yolk into a homogeneous dough and salt lightly.

❷ Rinse and clean spinach and blanch in boiling salted water. Immediately rinse under ice cold water, so spinach does not lose its colour. Drain in a colander and thoroughly squeeze dry using hands.

❸ Peel cloves of garlic and dice. Coarsely chop spinach. Stir together ricotta, remaining egg yolk, chopped garlic, salt and pepper. Then fold in spinach.

❹ Remove stem ends of tomatoes, cut an x in the top and briefly blanch in boiling water. Remove from water, rinse under ice cold water, peel off skin, cut into quarters, take out seeds and dice. In a skillet heat olive oil, add tomatoes and briefly rotate skillet. Season with salt, pepper and a pinch of sugar. Preheat oven to 180 °C.

❺ In a skillet heat some olive oil and bake 8 thin pancakes. Spread out pancakes next to each other and cover evenly with ricotta-spinach filling. Roll up and place into longish buttered baking dish. Distribute tomatoes and 2 types of cheese over crespelle. Bake in preheated oven for about 15 minutes.

Serves 4

120 g flour

200 ml milk

50 g liquid unsalted butter

2 whole eggs

2 egg yolks

Salt

500 g spinach leaves

3 garlic cloves

400 g ricotta cheese

Freshly ground black pepper

2 tomatoes

2 tablespoon olive oil

A pinch of sugar

Oil for baking pancakes

80 g grated Bel Paese cheese

1 tablespoon grated parmesan cheese

Butter for greasing baking dish

Crespelle Filled with Mustard-Pickled Fruits and Chicken Breast

The Italians like to preserve fruits like cherries, plums, peaches, figs, mirabelles and pears with sugar, glucose syrup, water and mustard oil. This adds a pleasant spiciness to the fruits, which goes well with poultry.

120 g flour

200 ml milk

2 whole eggs

1 egg yolk

50 g liquid unsalted butter

Salt

Oil for sautéing

2 chicken breasts, skin and
    bones removed

120 g mushrooms

2 tablespoons unsalted butter

80 g mixed mustard-pickled
    fruits, finely chopped

80 g Taleggio cheese

150 g crème fraîche

50 g cream

Freshly ground white pepper

❶ Knead flour, milk, whole eggs, egg yolk, butter and a pinch of salt into a smooth pancake dough and let rest for 30 minutes. In a skillet heat some olive oil and bake 8 crespelle (crisp pancakes) with a diameter of 15 cm. Allow to cool slightly on a cooling rack.

❷ Cut chicken breasts into bite-sized pieces and season with salt and pepper. Thinly slice mushrooms. Sauté chicken in 1 1/2 tablespoons butter until golden brown. Add mushrooms, briefly rotate and season with salt and pepper.

❸ Lightly butter an oven-proof oval dish. Spread out crespelle next to each other. Cover each with mustard-pickled fruits and chicken-mushroom-ragoût. Roll up and place into buttered dish. Preheat oven to 190 °C.

❹ Remove rind of Taleggio cheese, slice thinly and place on top of crespelle. Mix crème fraîche with cream, salt and pour over crespelle. Bake in preheated oven for about 20 minutes.

Serves 4

Crespelle with Spicy Salsiccia-Onion Sauce

Italian pork sausages have a very flavourful seasoning and taste especially delicious. Of course, you can also use pork chopped meat for the pancake filling.

❶ Knead flour, milk, whole eggs, egg yolk, butter and a pinch of salt into a smooth dough and let rest for 30 minutes. In a skillet heat some olive oil and bake 8 thin pancakes with a diameter of 15 cm. Allow to cool slightly on a cooling rack.

❷ Cut salsiccia into 1 cm pieces. Halve onions and cut into strips, chop garlic and sauté both in 2 tablespoons olive oil until soft and translucent.

❸ Add salsiccia and sprig of thyme and dust with paprika powder. Stir in tomato paste, add tomato pieces and simmer over low heat for 20 minutes. Season with salt, pepper and a pinch of sugar. Preheat oven to 190 °C.

❹ Fill crespelle with ragoût and place into a buttered dish. Top with slices of mozzarella and bake in preheated oven for about 20 minutes.

Serves 4

120 g flour

200 ml milk

2 whole eggs

1 egg yolk

50 g liquid unsalted butter

500 g Salsiccia (raw, coarse
    Italian sausages)

3 onions, peeled

2 garlic cloves, peeled

3 tablespoons olive oil

1 sprig of thyme

A pinch of paprika powder,
sweet

1 teaspoon tomato paste

1 small can peeled tomatoes
    in pieces

Butter for greasing baking dish

Salt

A pinch of sugar

Freshly ground black pepper

Crespelle Filled with Riccotta and Radicchio

120 g flour

200 ml milk

2 whole eggs

2 egg yolks

50 g liquid unsalted butter

Salt

650 g small heads of radicchio
   (red-leaf lettuce)

2 shallots

2 garlic cloves

1 tablespoon unsalted butter

A pinch of sugar

2 tablespoons Balsamic vinegar

2 sprigs of oregano

Freshly ground black pepper

250 g ricotta cheese

80 g gorgonzola cheese

Oil for baking pancake

Radicchio is more than just a beautiful looking, crisp salad. It tastes especially delicious braised or sautéed.

❶ For the pancake dough mix flour, milk, butter, whole eggs and 1 egg yolk into a homogeneous dough and salt lightly.

❷ Clean radicchio, halve, remove stalk and rinse in lukewarm water. It is best to dry salad in a salad spinner. Then tear leaves into small pieces.

❸ Peel shallots and garlic cloves, dice and sauté in butter until soft and translucent. Add radicchio, sauté briefly and caramelise with a pinch of sugar. Add Balsamic vinegar and cook over low heat until soft for about 5 minutes. Season with chopped oregano leaves, salt and pepper to taste

❹ Fold cooled radicchio and remaining egg yolk into ricotta and adjust seasoning with salt and pepper.

❺ In a medium-sized skillet (about 16 cm diameter) heat some olive oil and bake 8 thin pancakes. Preheat oven to 180 °C.

❻ Spread out pancakes on a board and cover evenly with ricotta-filling. Fold in half twice to form a triangle.

❼ Place crespelle into buttered baking dish and top evenly with sliced gorgonzola cheese. Bake in preheated oven for about 15 minutes.

Serves 4

Grilled Polenta with Cherry Tomatoes and Fontina Cheese

In Italy, polenta is cooked in a special polenta pot, which shows its importance. In order to cook real polenta you need some patience.

❶ Bring water to a boil in a wide pot. With a cooking spoon stir in cornmeal and simmer over low heat for about 45 minutes, whisking constantly.

❷ Lightly salt finished polenta and fill into a buttered dish. Let cool.

❸ Turn out cooled polenta and cut into 2 cm slices with a hot knife. Butter casserole dish with the remaining butter and layer in polenta slices like roofing tiles. Preheat oven to 190 °C.

❹ Wash cherry tomatoes and cut in half. Heat olive oil, briefly sauté cherry tomatoes and season with salt, pepper and a pinch of sugar.

❺ Evenly distribute tomatoes over polenta and sprinkle with grated Fontina cheese. Bake in preheated oven for about 20 minutes until golden brown.

Serves 4

3/4 l water

180 g cornmeal

Salt

1 tablespoon unsalted butter

16 cherry tomatoes

2 tablespoons olive oil

A pinch of sugar

Freshly ground black pepper

150 g Fontina cheese

Liquid Polenta with Gorgonzola Cheese and Butter

1 l water

150 g cornmeal

Salt

Freshly ground nutmeg

100 g gorgonzola cheese

20 g unsalted butter

❶ Bring water to a boil and slowly stir in cornmeal, whisking constantly. Simmer polenta for about 45 minutes, still whisking, and season with salt and nutmeg.

❷ Cut gorgonzola and butter into small pieces and stir into polenta before serving it in a deep bowl.

Serves 4

Polenta with Chanterelle Mushrooms and Rosemary Butter

1 l water

150 g cornstarch

Salt

Freshly ground nutmeg

350 g chanterelle mushrooms

1 bunch of spring onions

4 tablespoons unsalted butter

1 sprig of rosemary

Freshly ground black pepper

1 tablespoon parsley,
    finely chopped

❶ Prepare polenta following above recipe.

❷ Clean chanterelle mushrooms, rinse briefly, drain in a colander and dry on kitchen towel.

❸ Clean spring onions and diagonally cut into thin slices.

❹ Sauté chanterelle mushrooms in 2 tablespoons foamy butter. Pluck a few rosemary needles and set aside. Add rosemary sprig and spring onions to mushrooms and sauté with mushrooms over low heat for about 5 minutes. Remove rosemary sprig, add remaining butter and season with salt, pepper and a pinch of nutmeg. Finely chop rosemary needles and add to mushrooms with fresh parsley.

❺ Arrange polenta and mushroom-onion mixture on plates.

Serves 4

Prosecco Risotto with Sautéed Porcini Mushrooms

If you are one of the lucky ones who live near a forest you should go mushrooming yourself. Mushrooms you pick yourself always taste best.

❶ Clean mushrooms, slice not too thinly and set aside. Finely chop stalks.

❷ Peel 2 shallots and garlic, dice finely and briefly sauté in 2 tablespoons olive oil and butter. Add rice and sauté until soft and translucent. Add rosemary needles and porcini mushrooms, then pour in prosecco.

❸ Slowly add vegetable broth, one tablespoon at a time, while stirring, and cook rice al dente. Adjust seasoning with white pepper and nutmeg.

❹ Heat olive oil in a non-stick pan and sauté mushrooms until golden brown. Peel and dice remaining shallot, mix with garlic and parsley and add to risotto.

❻ Before serving stir in grated parmesan cheese.

Serves 4

250 g fresh porcini mushrooms

2 1/2 shallots

1 clove garlic

4 tablespoons olive oil

1 tablespoon unsalted butter

350 g risotto rice (arborio or vialone rice)

1/2 teaspoon rosemary needles, finely chopped

200 ml Prosecco

3/4 l vegetable stock

Salt

Freshly ground white pepper

Freshly ground nutmeg

A pinch of garlic, finely chopped

1 tablespoon parsley, chopped

80 g parmesan cheese

Spinach Risotto with White Truffles

600 g winter spinach

2 shallots, diced

2 garlic cloves, diced

2 tablespoons olive oil

2 tablespoons unsalted butter

300 g vialone rice (risotto rice)

200 ml dry white wine

About 3/4 l vegetable broth

Salt

Freshly ground white pepper

Freshly ground nutmeg

80 g grated young parmesan
   cheese

1 white truffle, about 40 g

Fall is truffle season and every gourmet gets excited. This is certainly not an every-day dish. But if you want to treat your palate once in a while, this dish will not disappoint you.

❶ Clean winter spinach and wash thoroughly. Blanch in boiling salted water for 4 minutes. Drain in a colander and rinse under ice cold water. Thoroughly squeeze dry and coarsely chop.

❷ Briefly sauté shallots and garlic in oil and 1 tablespoon butter until soft and translucent. Add rice, briefly sauté, then add white wine.

❸ Slowly add vegetable broth, one tablespoon at a time, while stirring, and cook rice al dente for about 15 minutes.

❹ Adjust seasoning with salt, white pepper and nutmeg.

❺ Shortly before serving, fold grated parmesan cheese, remaining cold butter and chopped spinach into rice and arrange on plates.

❻ Rub white truffles clean with kitchen towel or special truffle brush and, depending on taste, cut into thin slices or grate over risotto.

Serves 4

Pumpkin Risotto with Ricotta

Pumpkins are available in all shapes, colours and sizes. They have an intense flavour and their orange flesh is used in a variety of different ways, from main courses to desserts. You can purchase them whole or in individual portions. Smaller pumpkins have a harder flesh and need to be cooked a little longer.

❶ Finely dice pumpkin flesh and onions and sauté in 1 tablespoon heated butter. Sprinkle with sugar and add some water. Braise over low heat until soft, stirring from time to time. If necessary, pour in some more water occasionally. Pumpkin flesh should be very soft and dry. Finely purée with hand blender and season with salt and pepper.

❷ Sauté shallots and garlic in olive oil and 1 tablespoon butter until soft and translucent. Add rice, briefly sauté and pour in white wine.

❸ Add vegetable broth one tablespoon at a time and sauté until al dente for about 15 minutes, stirring constantly. Season with salt, white pepper and nutmeg.

❹ Shortly before serving, fold grated parmesan cheese, remaining cold butter and pumpkin mousse into rice.

❺ Arrange pumpkin risotto in deep plates. Place a dollop of ricotta cheese into the middle and drizzle with chili oil. Garnish with sautéed pumpkin slices.

Serves 4

400 g pumpkin flesh

1 peeled onion

3 tablespoons unsalted butter

A pinch of sugar

Salt

Freshly ground white pepper

2 shallots, diced

2 garlic cloves, diced

2 tablespoons olive oil

300 g vialone rice (risotto rice)

200 ml dry white wine

About 3/4 l vegetable broth

Freshly ground nutmeg

80 g grated young parmesan cheese

2 tablespoons ricotta cheese

Chili oil

10. Fish and Seafood

Branzino
Sautéed Bass with Parsley and Lemon

600 g whole bass

Salt

Freshly ground white pepper

1/2 bunch of flat-leaf parsley

2 sprigs of thyme

2 small fresh bay leaves

Flour for dusting

2 tablespoons olive oil

2 tablespoons capers

2 lemons

3 tablespoons unsalted butter

It is best to buy the bass kitchen-ready at the fishmonger. You can also use trout or seabream for this recipe.

❶ Rinse bass under running, cold water and especially wash inside of belly. Pat dry with kitchen paper.

❷ With a sharp knife make 3 to 4 parallel incisions on both sides (about 5 cm long) behind the head into skin (so bass cooks more evenly and the skin does not contract). Season bass with salt and pepper, inside and outside. Fill bass with a few parsley sprigs without the leaves, 1 sprig of thyme and 1 bay leaf. Lightly dust skin side of fish with flour. This turns skin nice and crisp during sautéing. Preheat oven to 180 °C.

❸ Heat oil in a large pan and sauté bass on both sides until crisp. Carefully turn fish after 3 minutes.

❹ Place pan with fish in preheated oven and bake for about 12 minutes until tender. Keep basting bass with juices, that issue from fish.

❺ In the meantime, coarsely chop capers. Peel lemon with a knife in such a way that all white skin is completely removed, then fillet lemons with a sharp knife. Tear parsley leaves from remaining sprig and chop coarsely.

❻ Remove fish from oven and pour out oil. Melt butter in a hot pan, add capers, lemon fillets, remaining thyme and bay leaf and finish with parsley. Season with salt and pepper. Arrange bass on a plate and drizzle with lemon-caper butter. Serve with fresh baguette.

Serves 2

Sautéed Monkfish with Fennel and Artichokes

❶ Clean fennel, halve and cut into 1 cm thick wedges. Peel away the outer hard leaves of the artichokes. Cut off the prickly points of the remaining leaves. Scrape out the fuzzy choke in the centre with a spoon. Immediately place artichokes in lemon water.

❷ Halve tomatoes. Cut monkfish in 2 cm thick medallions, season with salt and pepper and sauté in olive oil on both sides for about 3 minutes. Remove monkfish from pan and keep warm. Heat butter and sauté fennel and artichokes for about 3 minutes. Add tomatoes, fish stock and thyme and simmer for an additional 5 minutes. Finely crush fennel seeds with mortar and pestle. Adjust seasoning of vegetables with fennel. Arrange monkfish medallions on top of artichokes.

Serves 4

200 g fennel

8 young artichokes

1 lemon

200 g cherry tomatoes, peeled

600 g monkfish

Salt

Freshly ground white pepper

1 tablespoon olive oil

2 tablespoons unsalted butter

200 ml fish stock

2 sprigs of thyme

Cayenne pepper

1/2 teaspoon fennel seeds

Turbot with Leek and Fresh Tarragon

❶ Clean leek, halve and thoroughly wash under running water. Cut leek into 1 cm pieces. Cook potatoes in plenty of salted water until al dente and drain in a colander. Briefly sauté leek in 1 tablespoon butter, pour in fish stock and simmer for 5 minutes. Add potatoes and adjust seasoning with salt, pepper and mustard.

❷ Salt and pepper turbot fillets, lightly dust with flour and sauté in olive oil and remaining butter on both sides for about 3 minutes until golden brown. Lightly whip cream and fold into the hot leeks. Finish with finely chopped tarragon. Serve turbot with potato-leek vegetables.

Serves 4

2 stalks leek

500 g potatoes, peeled and diced

2 tablespoons unsalted butter

100 ml fish stock

Salt

Freshly ground white pepper

Flour for dusting

1 teaspoon hot mustard

500 g turbot fillets

1 tablespoon olive oil

100 g cream

2 sprigs of tarragon

Sautéed Prawns with Garlic–Herb Butter

24 whole prawns
   (with heads and shells)
2 garlic cloves
3 tablespoons unsalted butter
1/2 bunch of chives
2 tablespoons parsley, chopped
Salt
Freshly ground black pepper
1/2 teaspoon grated peel of
   1 organically grown lemon

Of course, prawns taste best cooked in their shells. During the cooking process, the shells transfer all their flavour to the meat. Even in elegant restaurants, prawns or crayfish are served without utensils. They are served with a small dish with lemon water, so you can wash your hands at the table.

❶ Wash and dry prawns. Peel garlic, cut in half and slice thinly. Pre-heat oven to 190 °C.

❷ Grease oven-proof dish lightly with butter. Season prawns with salt and pepper, place into dish and bake in preheated oven for about 10 minutes.

❸ In the meantime, thinly chop chives. Beat remaining butter until foamy using a hand blender and mix with garlic, parsley and chives. Season with salt, pepper and grated lemon peel.

❹ Remove prawns from oven and cover with herb butter. Bake for an additional 5 minutes in the oven under high heat from above. It is best to serve prawns in the dish right from the oven. Serve with fresh baguette and lemon wedges.

Serves 4

Mussels au Gratin with Herbs

You don't need to be great cook to prepare mussels. The only important thing is to use very fresh mussels. If mussels do not open during cooking, do not eat them!

❶ Remove beards, stones or any other dirt from mussels and scrub thoroughly with a brush under running water.

❷ Heat olive oil in a wide pot, add sliced shallots and bay leaves and sauté for 4 minutes until soft and translucent. Add wet mussels to onions and cover pot with a lid.

❸ Allow mussels to open, moving pot from time to time so mussels do not stick to the bottom. Drain mussels in a colander.

4 Allow mussels to cool slightly, open and remove mussel from shell. Only use mussels that have opened by themselves during cooking. Place mussel back into its half shell.

5 Tear off parsley leaves and chop finely. Peel garlic and chop finely as well.

Serves 4

1 kg – 1.2 kg blue mussels
2 shallots, sliced
2 bay leaves
100 g grated baguette
100 g unsalted butter
1 bunch of flat-leaf parsley
2 garlic cloves, finely chopped
3 tablespoons olive oil
Salt
Freshly ground black pepper
Coarse sea salt

❻ Beat butter with a hand blender until foamy, add grated baguette and mix together well. Season with finely chopped parsley, garlic, salt and pepper.

❼ Sprinkle coarse sea salt over the bottom of an oven-proof dish.

❽ Spread herb crust onto individual mussels and evenly distribute onto sea salt. The salt helps mussels to set in the dish and prevents the shells from burning. Bake mussels at high heat from above in the oven or in a grill until golden brown.

❾ These mussels are a delicious hot appetizer. Serve with fresh baguette and a glass of dry white wine.

Anchovies in Parsley–Butter with Tomatoes and Chopped Egg

To remove head and bones from anchovies is not that difficult if you know how to go about it. Just try it or let your local fish-monger show you.

❶ Cut belly of anchovy open and carefully pull out the head together with the back bone. Thoroughly rinse anchovies under running cold water and pat try with kitchen paper.

❷ Remove radicchio from stalk and cut head into 1 cm slices.

❸ Lightly dredge anchovies in flour on both sides and sauté in hot oil until golden brown. Season with salt and pepper, remove from skillet and drain on kitchen paper.

❹ Remove stem ends of tomatoes, cut an x in the top and blanch in boiling water for 2 minutes. Rinse under ice cold water, peel off skin, cut into quarters, take out seeds and dice.

❺ Chop eggs and mix with Balsamic vinegar and olive oil. Add tomatoes and season with salt, pepper and sugar.

❻ Arrange individual radicchio portions on plates, place anchovies on top and drizzle with tomato-egg vinaigrette. Tear basil leaves into small pieces and garnish anchovies.

Serves 4

24 fresh anchovies
1 radicchio
Flour for dusting
Oil
Salt
Freshly ground black pepper
3 tomatoes
2 hard-boiled eggs, peeled
3 tablespoons Balsamic vinegar
6 tablespoons olive oil
A pinch of sugar
A few fresh basil leaves

Stuffed Calamari with Tomato-Clam Sauce

4 octopus tubes (120 g each),
    kitchen-ready, head removed

60 g raisins

1 cup of black tea, lukewarm

50 g pine nuts

1 tomato

130 g ricotta cheese

2 egg yolks

80 g grated baguette

1/2 bunch of flat-leaf parsley,
    chopped

Salt

Freshly ground black pepper

2 tablespoons olive oil

2 round red peppers, quartered
    and seeded

80 g clams, shelled (vongole)

2 sprigs of oregano

Have your local fishmonger clean and prepare squids. Tubes can be stuffed with a variety of fillings, e.g. mussels or spinach-ricotta paste.

❶ Thoroughly wash squid tubes under running cold water and pat inside and outside dry.

❷ Soak raisins in tea. Tea has a neutral flavour and preserves the natural flavours of raisins. Roast pine nuts in a skillet without oil until golden brown, allow to cool and chop coarsely.

❸ Remove stem ends of tomatoes, cut an x in the top and briefly blanch in boiling water. Rinse under ice cold water, peel off skin, cut into quarters, take out seeds and dice.

❹ Mix ricotta cheese, egg yolk, grated baguette, some parsley, pine nuts and drip-dried raisins together and season with salt and pepper. Stuff mixture into tubes, close with a wooden skewer and season with salt and pepper. Preheat oven to 180 °C.

❺ Briefly sauté tubes in heated olive oil on all sides. Add peppers and bake in preheated oven for about 30 minutes until done. From time to time pour some water over squids. A few minutes before baking is finished, add clams and heat in cooking liquids. Arrange squid tubes with peppers on plates and pour clam sauce over it. If desired, sprinkle with chopped parsley or oregano leaves. Serve with crisp baguette.

Serves 4

Grilled Swordfish with Olives and Capers

2 slices of swordfish, 500 g each

salt

Freshly ground black pepper

2 garlic cloves, peeled

80 g pitted black olives

2 tablespoons capers

1 tablespoon olive oil

2 tablespoons cold unsalted
butter

Lemon juice

1/2 bunch of flat-leaf parsley

The consistency and flavour of fresh swordfish are reminiscent of tender veal. It is a true alternative for meat lovers. Swordfish has firm meat and is especially suitable for grilling and sautéing and goes well with strong spices.

❶ Season swordfish with salt and pepper and sauté in lightly oiled grill pan on both sides for about 6 minutes.

❷ In the meantime, thinly slice garlic cloves, halve oranges and coarsely chop capers.

❸ Drizzle swordfish with olive oil and remove from pan after an additional 3 minutes. Place onto preheated platter.

❹ Place cold butter into pan, add olives and capers, toss briefly and season with lemon juice, salt and pepper. Finish with parsley and pour over swordfish.

❺ Serve swordfish with fresh baguette and olive bread. A tannin-rich glass of red wine tastes delicious with this dish.

Serves 4

11. Meat Dishes

Involtini Veal Rolls Stuffed with Pumpkin and Amaretti

400 g pumpkin, peeled and
seeded

Red and yellow pepper, 1 each,
halved and seeded

1 onion, peeled

2 tablespoons unsalted butter

1/4 l vegetable stock

A pinch of sugar

4 tablespoons baguette, grated

8 Amaretti

1 egg

Salt

Freshly ground black pepper

1 tablespoon honey

6 veal cutlets from plate,
100 g each

6 slices of Parma ham

2 shallots, peeled and diced

2 sprigs of thyme

2 fresh bay leaves

Pumpkins in all their different colours, shapes and sizes, stacked up high at the farmers' markets, are a beautiful sight in the fall. But pumpkins not only look decorative but can be used in a variety of different ways in the kitchen: preserved as sweet-and-sour vegetables, as a hearty soup or as pumpkin risotto – there are endless possibilities.

❶ Finely dice pumpkin, red and yellow pepper and onion. Heat 1 tablespoon butter and sauté diced onions until soft and translucent. Add pumpkin and sauté over low heat for an additional 5 minutes. Cook until soft over low heat while constantly pouring vegetable broth over pumpkin. All the liquid should have evaporated.

❷ Briefly sauté peppers in the remaining foamy butter and caramelise with sugar. Stir cooled pumpkin mousse with diced peppers, baguette, crushed amaretti and one egg into a homogeneous mixture, season with salt and pepper and finish with honey. Preheat oven to 180 °C.

❸ Pound veal cutlet flat with a meat pounder, season with salt and pepper and cover with slices of Parma ham. Spread pumpkin mixture evenly onto cutlet, roll up and secure the end with tooth picks. Place veal rolls into buttered oven-proof dish and add diced shallots, sprigs of thyme and bay leaves. Add some water. Braise in preheated oven for about 1 hour. During braising, keep turning veal rolls over and baste with meat juice from time to time. Serve with rice or salted potatoes.

Serves 6-8

Stuffings

Here are a few ideas for fancy veal roll stuffings that are fast and easy to prepare.

Hearty-Spicy Stuffing

Remove skin from raw sausages and finish paste with chopped parsley and sautéed diced bacon. Pound veal cutlets flat, fill them with mixture and braise.

Poultry Liver Stuffing

Pass poultry liver through coarse setting of meat grinder. Cut dry baguette into cubes and mix with egg, liver, sautéed onions and finely chopped sage leaves. Fill veal cutlets with mixture and braise.

Spinach Stuffing

Mix blanched spinach with sautéed garlic, onions, egg and ricotta into a homogeneous mixture. Stir in grated baguette, freshly ground parmesan cheese and diced ham. Fill veal rolls with mixture and braise.

Veal Liver with Raisins and Pine Nuts

500 g veal liver, kitchen-ready

500 g white onions

1 tablespoon olive oil

1 sprig of thyme

Salt

Sugar

Flour for dusting

2 tablespoons unsalted butter

Freshly ground black pepper

2 tablespoons Balsamic vinegar

200 ml veal sauce

80 g raisins, soaked in lukewarm
water

80 g pine nuts, roasted

1 tablespoon flat-leaf parsley,
chopped

In Italy, this dish is served with polenta. But veal liver also tastes good with mashed potatoes or set on top of a bed of marinated mixed greens served with oil-roasted slices of bread.

❶ Thinly slice veal liver and onions. Sauté onions in olive oil until golden brown. Add plucked thyme leaves and season with salt and a pinch of sugar. Pour onions through strainer and catch olive oil in a dish.

❷ Lightly dust sliced veal liver with flour. Heat 1 tablespoon butter and the olive oil from the dish in a non-stick pan and sauté sliced liver on both sides over high heat. Season with salt and pepper. Then pour in vinegar followed by veal sauce. Add onion slices and cook until sauce thickens. Stir in drip-dried raisins and pine nuts and finish with parsley. Serve immediately.

Serves 2

Ossobuco alla milanese Sliced Veal Hocks with Gremolata Butter

Most important for this dish are patience and slow cooking. This is the only way to bring out its full flavour. Spicy gremolata butter adds a fresh taste to the sliced hocks.

❶ Cut carrots, celery and onions into 1/2 cm cubes. Finely chop garlic. Tie kitchen string around sliced veal hocks. Lightly dust with flour, season with salt and pepper and sauté in a roasting pan in heated olive oil on all sides until golden brown. Preheat oven to 170 °C.

❷ Take out meat. Add butter, finely chopped vegetables, garlic and tomato paste to cooking liquids and heat for about 5 minutes. Pour in white wine, add sliced hocks and braise covered in preheated oven for about 2 1/2 hours.

❸ Remove stem end of tomatoes, cut an x in the top and briefly blanch them in boiling water. Rinse under ice cold water, peel off skin, cut into quarters and take out seeds. After sliced hocks have braised for 30 minutes, add tomatoes, thyme and bay leaf and pour in veal stock. From time to time pour veal stock and vegetables over meat.

❹ For gremolata finely chop all ingredients with the butter and season with salt and pepper. Also season sauce with salt and pepper. Arrange sliced hocks on plates and cover with gremolata butter. Saffron risotto is the traditional side dish.

Serves 4

3 carrots, peeled

4 stalks celery

2 onions, peeled

3 garlic cloves, peeled

4 slices of veal hocks, 400 g each

Flour for dusting

Salt

Freshly ground black pepper

3 tablespoons olive oil

1 tablespoon unsalted butter

1 tablespoon tomato paste

1/4 l dry white wine

4 ripe large tomatoes

2 sprigs of thyme

1 bay leaf

1/2 l veal stock

For gremolata:

1/2 teaspoon grated lemon peel

1/2 teaspoon grated orange peel

1/2 teaspoon caraway seeds

2 garlic cloves, peeled

1 tablespoon flat-leaf parsley

1 teaspoon marjoram leaves

2 tablespoons unsalted butter

Small Veal Schnitzel with Porcini Mushrooms and Thyme

Mushroomers who know where to find the delicious porcini mushrooms never like to give away their secret spots. It is important when picking to carefully cut off mushrooms so a new mushroom can grow in its place. Mushroom picking is a passion. Once you found one it's hard to stop.

600 g veal fillet in one piece

1 tablespoon unsalted butter

2 shallots, peeled and diced

2 sprigs of thyme

1/4 l veal sauce

4 porcini mushrooms, cleaned
　　and quartered

Salt

Freshly ground black pepper

Freshly ground nutmeg

1 tablespoon flat-leaf parley,
finely chopped

❶ Cut veal fillet into 12 slices and sauté in 1 tablespoon hot butter on both sides for about 3 minutes. Remove veal slices from skillet, wrap in aluminium foil and keep warm. Briefly sauté half of the shallots and plucked thyme leaves in the same skillet. Pour in veal sauce and simmer slowly for 5 minutes.

❷ Heat 1 tablespoon butter in a second skillet and sauté porcini mushrooms on all sides for about 4 minutes. Add remaining onions and season with salt, pepper and a pinch of nutmeg. Shortly before serving, finish with parsley.

❸ Place veal slices with their juices in the sauce, season with salt and pepper and serve with porcini mushrooms and oven-roasted potatoes.

Serves 4

Saltimbocca alla Romana
Veal Schnitzel with Ham and Sage

❶ Pound veal schnitzel with the flat side of a meat pounder until flat and season with salt and pepper. Layer veal schnitzel with Parma ham and one sage leaf each and pin to meat with a toothpick. Sauté veal schnitzel in 1 tablespoon butter on both sides for about 3 minutes, remove and keep warm.

❷ Add white wine to cooking liquids, then pour in veal stock and cook until sauce thickens. Stir 2 tablespoons of cold butter into sauce. Adjust seasoning again with salt and pepper and place meat slices into sauce. Briefly rotate and serve with baguette.

Serves 4

8 thin slices of veal schnitzel,
    70 g each
Salt
Freshly ground black pepper
8 thin slices of Parma ham
8 large sage leaves
3 tablespoons unsalted butter
1/8 l dry white wine
1/8 l veal stock

Larded Veal Liver with Bacon and Rosemary

❶ Cut bacon into 1 cm wide and 2 cm long strips. Lard sliced veal liver with bacon strips about 4 cm apart from each other using a larding needle.

❷ Slice shallots and garlic. Lightly dust sliced liver with flour and sauté in hot butter on both sides for about 4 minutes. Add shallots and rosemary and sauté briefly. Remove liver from pan and add veal stock to cooking liquids. Simmer slowly for 5 minutes. Season with salt and pepper, add sliced liver to sauce, rotate briefly and serve with mashed potatoes.

Serves 4

200 g streaky bacon in one piece
8 slices of veal liver, 80 g each
3 shallots, peeled
1 clove garlic, peeled
Flour for dusting
2 tablespoons unsalted butter
2 sprigs of rosemary
1/4 l veal juice
Salt
Freshly ground black pepper

Braised Rabbit with Tomatoes and Artichokes

Instead of the artichokes you can braise fennel with the rabbit just as well. True gourmets actually only braise the meat with the vegetables to intensify the flavour of the vegetables, especially the garlic.

❶ It is best to have your local butcher cut the rabbit into pieces. Season with salt and pepper.

❷ Peel away the outer hard leaves of the artichokes. Cut off the prickly points of the remaining leaves. Scrape out the fuzzy choke in the centre with a spoon. Halve artichokes and immediately place them in cold lemon water.

❸ Remove stem ends of tomatoes and lengthwise cut into quarters. Cut carrots and celery into ca. 5 cm pieces. Cut onions into coarse cubes. Preheat oven to 170 °C.

❹ Cover inside of roasting pan with soft butter. Evenly distribute rabbit, vegetables, onions and garlic in pan and braise in preheated oven for about 1 1/2 hours. From time to time, add a dash of water. Occasionally turn rabbit and baste with meat juices. This will keep the meat from drying out and it stays juicy. It is best to serve rabbit in the roasting pan with oven-roasted potatoes.

Serves 4

One rabbit, kitchen-ready,
   about 1.6 kg
Salt
Freshly ground black pepper
4 artichokes
1 lemon
2 plum tomatoes
2 carrots, peeled
1 stalk celery
2 onions, peeled
1 tablespoon unsalted butter
6 garlic cloves, unpeeled and
   pressed
2 sprigs of thyme
1 sprig of rosemary

Stuffed Guinea Fowl with Grape Sauce

4 guinea fowl breasts

4 slices of toast, diced

3 tablespoons pine nuts

4 tablespoons unsalted butter

1 onion, peeled and diced

2 sprigs of mint

1 whole egg

1 egg yolk

Salt

Freshly ground black pepper

Freshly ground nutmeg

For grape sauce:

200 g white grapes

2 tablespoons sugar

50 ml white Port wine

200 ml poultry stock

1 teaspoon cornstarch

1 tablespoon cold butter, diced

❶ Wash guinea fowl breasts and pat dry with kitchen towel. Remove rind of toast and cut into small cubes. Roast pine nuts in a skillet without oil until golden brown, allow to cool slightly and chop coarsely.

❷ Roast diced toast in 1 tablespoon butter until golden brown. Beat 2 tablespoons soft butter with a hand blender until foamy. Sauté onions in a non-stick pan with little butter until soft and translucent and allow to cool. Coarsely chop plucked mint leaves and stir into the bread mixture with pine nuts, onions, whole egg and egg yolk. Season with salt, pepper and a pinch of nutmeg.

❸ Fill bread mixture into piping bag with a large tip and fill guinea fowls underneath the skin with mixture. Do not stuff guinea fowls too much, otherwise skin can burst during roasting.

❹ Halve grapes and remove skin and seeds. Lightly caramelise sugar, add grapes and pour in Port wine. Allow liquid to evaporate completely, add poultry stock and simmer for an additional 5 minutes. Stir cornstarch together with some water and use mixture to bind boiling grape sauce. Preheat oven to 180 °C.

❺ Season guinea fowl breasts with salt and pepper. Heat remaining butter in a non-stick skillet and briefly sauté breasts on skin side. Bake in preheated oven for about 12 minutes, basting guinea fowls with liquid that issues from the meat. Heat grape sauce and finish with cold butter flakes. Cut guinea fowls open and serve with grape sauce and fresh baguette.

Serves 4

Quails Sautéed with Garlic and Rosemary

In addition, quails can be stuffed with marinated Armagnac prunes. The fruit juice complements fresh rosemary and garlic well. If you are very hungry, simply double the amount of quails.

❶ Wash quails and pat dry with kitchen towel. Rub inside and outside of quail with salt and pepper. Preheat oven to 200 °C.

❷ Press garlic in its peel and place with rosemary, bay leaves and quails into buttered roasting pan.

❸ Bake in preheated oven for about 20 minutes. Keep pouring meat juice over quails. This will turn the skin crisp and the meat stays juicy.

❹ Remove quails from roasting pan and keep warm. Add Port wine and poultry stock to cooking liquids and simmer until sauce thickens. Stir in remaining cold butter and season with salt and pepper. Serve quails with oven-roasted potatoes and poultry sauce.

Press roasted garlic easily out of its skin and enjoy – it is absolutely delicious.

Serves 4

4 meaty quails, kitchen-ready

8 garlic cloves

1 sprig rosemary

2 small bay leaves

50 ml Port wine

100 ml poultry stock

30 g unsalted butter

Salt

Freshly ground white pepper

Chicken with Figs and Honey

4 chicken breasts, bones
   removed

Salt

Freshly ground black pepper

2 tablespoons unsalted butter

2 sprigs of thyme

4 fresh figs

1 tablespoon wild honey

4 cl Calvados

1/4 l chicken stock

200 g cream

Figs with their sweet taste are not only used for desserts – they are more and more loved in hearty cuisine as well. These flavourful and healthy fruits taste especially good with poultry.

❶ Preheat oven to 180 °C. Season chicken breasts with salt and pepper. Heat half the butter and briefly sauté breasts on skin side. Bake in preheated oven for 15 minutes. Keep basting with cooking liquids. After 5 minutes of baking, add 1 sprig of thyme.

❷ Halve figs and briefly sauté in remaining butter. Drizzle with honey and caramelise.

❸ Remove chicken breasts from skillet, wrap in aluminium foil and keep warm in turned-off oven.

❹ Mix cooking liquids with Calvados, add stock and simmer for about 5 minutes. Stir in cream and cook until sauce thickens. Finish with remaining plucked thyme leaves and season with salt and pepper.

❺ Arrange chicken breast with caramelised figs and Calvados sauce on plates and serve with boiled rice.

Serves 4

Veal Tail Ragoût with Polenta

2 veal tails, 400 g each

Salt

Freshly ground black pepper

2 tablespoons unsalted butter

1 onion, peeled

1 clove garlic, peeled

1 carrot, peeled

1 parsley root, peeled

1/2 l stock

1/2 lemon, organically grown

1 sprig of thyme

For polenta:

About 1/2 l water

2 tablespoons olive oil

150 g polenta semolina

Salt

Since veal tail is very tender, it tastes best if prepared as naturally as possible. A piece of lemon peel, garlic and fresh thyme add a Mediterranean flavour to this dish. Polenta or simply fresh baguette make good side dishes for veal tail ragoût.

❶ It is best to have your local butcher cut veal tail into individual portions.

❷ Season veal tail pieces with salt and pepper. Heat butter and sauté meat pieces on all sides. Dice onions, garlic, carrot and parsley root and add to veal tail. Sauté together for an additional 5 minutes and pour in some stock. Preheat oven to 180 °C.

❸ Peel off a piece of lemon peel with a knife or a potato peeler and add to stock with thyme.

❹ Cover and cook veal tail in preheated oven for about 2 1/2 hours. Keep basting with stock.

❺ For the polenta, heat water and olive oil and stir in polenta semolina one tablespoon at a time. Allow to cook for about 40 minutes over low heat, whisking continuously. Season with salt.

❻ Squeeze out one lemon half and adjust ragoût seasoning with lemon juice. Season with salt and pepper if necessary and serve with polenta.

Serves 4

Chestnut-Walnut-Crusted Leg of Wild Boar

Did you buy too many chestnuts? No problem: they taste great by themselves, oven-roasted and still hot, on cold winter days with a glass of full-bodied red wine

❶ Preheat oven to 180 °C. Season leg of wild boar with salt and pepper. Heat oil in a roasting pan and briefly sauté meat on all sides over high heat. Add finely chopped vegetables, onions and garlic and roast in preheated oven for about 2 1/2 hours.

❷ After 30 minutes, add tomato paste, briefly roast with meat, then pour in a dash of red wine. Repeat procedure twice. Add game stock, 1 tablespoon at a time.

❸ Finely crush bay leaves, pepper and pimento corns and juniper berries with mortar and pestle and add to sauce. Keep basting leg with meat juices.

❹ Cut an x in the flat side of chestnut shells, place on baking sheet and bake in oven until shell cracks. Allow to cool slightly, then peel. Coarsely chop chestnuts in food processor. Mix with grated baguette, liquid butter and honey and season with cinnamon and ground cloves.

❺ About 30 minutes before roasting is done, lightly spread chestnut paste over leg of wild boar and keep baking. Bind sauce with vegetable paste and season with salt and pepper. Gnocchi or sautéed potato medallions are good side dishes.

Serves 4

1 kg boneless leg of wild boar

Salt

Freshly ground black pepper

2 tablespoons oil

1 carrot, peeled

1/4 celery root, peeled

2 onions, peeled

2 garlic cloves

1 tablespoon tomato paste

1/4 l red wine

1/2 l game stock

2 bay leaves

5 black peppercorns

4 pimento corns

5 juniper berries

80 g grated baguette

12 maroni (Italian chestnuts)

2 tablespoons walnuts

50 g unsalted butter

2 tablespoons honey

A pinch of cinnamon

A pinch of ground cloves

Piccata milanese
Veal Schnitzel in Cheese Dough with Tomato Sauce

1/2 l tomato sauce
   (see recipe on page 44)
400 g veal schnitzels from plate
Salt
Freshly ground black pepper
4 eggs
100 g grated parmesan cheese
4 tablespoons flour
Clarified butter for sautéing
Some fresh basil leaves

The Italian version of Viennese Schnitzel is not only loved by children. You can also substitute turkey for veal.

❶ Prepare tomato sauce following the recipe on page 44.

❷ Cut veal schnitzels in half and season with salt and pepper. Break eggs over a deep plate and beat with fork. Distribute parmesan and flour into 2 deep plates. Dredge veal schnitzels in flour, eggs and parmesan cheese (in that order). Press breading lightly to make sure it adheres to meat.

❸ Heat 2 tablespoons clarified butter in a non-stick skillet and slowly sauté veal schnitzels on both sides until golden brown. Remove from skillet and drain on kitchen paper.

❹ Finish tomato sauce with finely torn basil leaves and arrange on plates with sautéed veal schnitzels. The classic side dish for "Piccata milanese" is spaghetti.

Different possibility for preparation of cheese dough: Mix together 3 eggs, 4 tablespoons grated parmesan cheese and 2 tablespoons flour and season with salt and pepper. Dredge seasoned schnitzel in dough and sauté in hot clarified butter on both sides until golden brown.

Serves 4

Tagliata
Entrecôte on White Bean Salad with Arugula

The combination of grilled meat, hard cooking beans, arugula and olive oil is irresistible for gourmets. Add a glass of Chianti, some crisp ciabatta bread – what more could you possibly want? Tagliata can be served as an appetizer or a main course.

❶ Soak white beans in plenty of lukewarm water, preferably overnight. Drain in a colander and briefly sauté in 1 tablespoon heated olive oil. Add water, thyme and bay leaf and simmer beans over low heat until soft.

❷ Drain cooked beans in a colander and marinate in 5 tablespoons olive oil and Balsamic vinegar. Season with salt, pepper and sugar and finish with chopped walnuts.

❸ Season entrecôte with salt and pepper and sauté in a grill pan on both sides for 6 to 8 minutes, depending upon desired temperature of beef. Remove from pan, wrap in aluminium foil and let rest for 5 minutes.

❹ Mix bean salad with cleaned, rinsed and well dried arugula leaves and arrange on plates.

❺ Remove meat from aluminium foil and cut into thin slices using a sharp knife. Distribute individual portions onto prepared plates and drizzle with cooking liquid from pan. Season with coarse pepper if desired. A lemon wedge adds a fresh note to the Tagliata.

Serves 6

2 entrecôtes, 400 g each
150 g white beans, dried
6 tablespoons olive oil
1.6 l water
2 sprigs of thyme
1 bay leaf
1 bunch of arugula
2 tablespoons Balsamic vinegar
Salt
A pinch of sugar
Freshly ground black pepper
2 tablespoons walnuts, finely chopped

Stuffed Baby Goat with Stinging Nettles and Potatoes

1 leg of baby goat

200 g feta cheese

1 egg yolk

2 tablespoons cream cheese

2 tablespoons freshly grated
baguette

2 tablespoons pine nuts, roasted

2 garlic cloves, finely chopped

1 small bunch of stinging nettles

1/2 bunch of parsley

Salt

Freshly ground black pepper

2 carrots, peeled

1 onion, peeled

500 g small potatoes, that
    remain firm when boiled

2 tablespoons olive oil

6 garlic cloves, unpeeled and
    pressed

1 teaspoon tomato paste

1/4 l red wine

1/2 l poultry stock

❶ It is best to have your local butcher remove the bones from the leg of baby goat and chop them into walnut-sized pieces.

❷ Finely dice feta cheese. Add egg yolk, cream cheese and grated baguette and thoroughly mix together. Work in pine nuts, chopped garlic cloves and finely chopped parsley and stinging nettles. Season with salt and pepper.

❸ Rub inside and outside of leg of baby goat with salt and pepper and stuff with cheese mixture. Loosely sew opening shut with kitchen string. Make sure not to tie string too tightly, so stuffing does not come out during roasting. Preheat oven to 180 °C.

❹ Cut carrots and onions into coarse pieces. Peel potatoes. Brush roasting pan with olive oil and evenly distribute carrots, onions, chopped bones, potatoes and garlic cloves in pan. Arrange leg of baby goat on vegetables and roast in preheated oven for about 2 1/2 hours. Keep basting with meat juices.

❺ After 45 minutes of roasting, add tomato paste, briefly roast, then add a dash of red wine. Allow liquid to evaporate completely and repeat this procedure twice. Add poultry stock and roast until finished.

❻ Remove leg of baby goat from roasting pan and let rest briefly. Remove bones from sauce and season sauce with salt and pepper. Cut leg into slices and serve with potatoes, vegetables and sauce.

Serves 6

Roasted Saddle of Lamb Wrapped in Bacon with Leek and Truffles

For truffle lovers, this saddle of lamb will be the culinary highlight of the year. It is not an everyday meal, but once a year you should treat yourself to this luxury.

❶ Season saddle of lamb with salt and pepper. Finely chop a few rosemary needles and plucked thyme leaves and sprinkle over saddle of lamb. Evenly wrap saddle with sliced bacon. Preheat oven to 180 °C.

❷ Clean stalks of leek, halve and wash thoroughly. Remove hard, dark green leaf tips. Cut light part into 6 cm long pieces and blanch in boiling salted water for 5 minutes. Drain and rinse under ice cold water.

❸ Sauté saddle of lamb in non-stick skillet in olive oil and 1 tablespoon butter over medium heat on all sides. Add remaining sprig of rosemary and pressed garlic cloves and roast in preheated oven for about 20 minutes. Keep basting saddle with meat juices.

❹ Briefly sauté leek in remaining butter, add vegetable stock and simmer for 5 minutes. Season with salt, pepper and nutmeg. Arrange saddle of lamb on leek. Finely grate truffles with a truffle grater over meat and enjoy with fresh baguette.

Serves 4

1 kg saddle of milk lamb, trimmed (have butcher prepare saddle so bones protrude from meat)
Salt
Freshly ground black pepper
2 sprigs of rosemary
1 sprig of thyme
200 g breakfast bacon, thinly sliced
2 stalks leek
1 tablespoon olive oil
1 tablespoon unsalted butter
2 garlic cloves, unpeeled and pressed
Freshly ground nutmeg
1 white truffle (30 g), cleaned

Sautéed Lamb Cutlets with Tomatoes and Rosemary Oil

8 double lamb cutlets

2 sprigs of rosemary

2 garlic cloves, peeled

6 tablespoons olive oil

4 tomatoes

Salt

Freshly ground black pepper

A pinch of sugar

A few sprigs of flat-leaf parsley

Simple but amazingly delicious!

❶ Wash lamb cutlets and pat dry. Marinate with some rosemary needles, finely chopped garlic and 4 tablespoons olive oil, preferably overnight. Cover with clingfilm and chill.

❷ Remove stem end of tomatoes and cut an x in the top. Briefly blanch them in boiling water for 2 minutes, rinse under ice cold water, peel off skin, cut into quarters, take out seeds and dice.

❸ Heat 2 tablespoons oil from marinade in a grill pan. Season lamb cutlets with salt and pepper and grill on both sides for about 3 minutes. Also grill sprig of rosemary with cutlets.

❹ Briefly sauté diced tomatoes in 2 tablespoons olive oil and season with salt, pepper and a pinch of sugar. Coarsely chop plucked parsley leaves and add to tomatoes.

❺ Serve sautéed lamb cutlets with tomato ragoût and fresh baguette.

Zucchini-tomato vegetables also go very well with this dish: Slice large zucchini and 4 tomatoes and place in greased casserole dish. Season with garlic, rosemary and coarse salt, drizzle with olive oil and bake in oven at 180 °C for about 30 minutes.

Serves 4

Trippa alla parmigiana
Tripe in Tomato Sauce and Parmesan

Not for everyone, but many gourmets consider it to be a real delicacy. Pre-order tripe at your local butcher ahead of time. It only tastes good when it is very fresh.

❶ Cut tripe into 5 cm long and 1/2 cm strips. Finely dice onion and finely chop garlic.

❷ Heat 2 tablespoons olive oil. Sauté onions and garlic until soft and translucent, add tripe and together sauté over low heat for an additional 5 minutes, stirring constantly.

❸ Add white wine and pour in tomato sauce. Cover tripe and simmer for about 45 minutes, stirring occasionally. After about 20 minutes add herbs. Season with salt, pepper and cayenne pepper.

❹ Serve tripe in deep plates and sprinkle with parmesan cheese. A few drops of good olive oil and freshly ground black pepper add a final touch to tripe. Serve with Italian baguette or salted boiled potatoes.

Serves 4

700 g tripe (cleaned by butcher)
2 onions, peeled
2 garlic cloves, peeled
2 tablespoons olive oil
200 ml white wine
1/4 l tomato sauce
   (see recipe on page 44)
1 sprig of rosemary
2 sprigs of thyme
Salt
Freshly ground black pepper
Cayenne pepper
Freshly ground parmesan cheese

Spezzatino di vitello
Veal Ragoût with Zucchini and Mushrooms

800 g veal shoulder

3 onions

2 stalks celery

1 carrot, peeled

2 garlic cloves, peeled

400 g potatoes, that remain firm
    when boiled

Salt

Freshly ground black pepper

Cayenne pepper

6 tablespoons olive oil

1/4 l white wine

1/4 l veal stock

2 sprigs of thyme

4 tomatoes

100 g small mushrooms

80 g chanterelle mushrooms

1 large zucchini

1 shallot, peeled

A few sprigs of flat-leaf parsley

1 peperoncino, dried

❶ Cut veal shoulder into 1 cm thick cubes. Finely dice onions, celery and carrots. Finely chop garlic. Wash, peel and dice potatoes.

❷ Season veal shoulder with salt, pepper and a pinch of cayenne pepper. In a deep roasting pan heat 4 tablespoons olive oil and sauté meat cubes until golden brown. Add onions, celery, carrots, garlic and potatoes and sauté together for 5 minutes. Add white wine, pour in veal stock and add sprigs of thyme. Cover and simmer over medium heat for about 40 minutes.

❸ In the meantime, remove stem end of tomatoes, cut an x in the top and briefly blanch them in boiling water. Rinse under ice cold water, peel off skin, cut into quarters, take out seeds and dice. Add to meat after it has simmered for 30 minutes.

❹ Rinse mushrooms and chanterelle mushrooms and rub clean with a kitchen towel. Halve mushrooms, depending upon size, and dice zucchini.

❺ Heat 2 tablespoons of olive oil in a skillet and briefly sauté diced zucchini, mushrooms and diced shallot one after the other. Sauté together over low heat for 4 minutes. Season with salt and pepper and finish with plucked, finely chopped parsley leaves.

❻ Season veal ragoût with salt and pepper and, depending on taste, adjust seasoning with ground peperoncino. Serve with zucchini vegetables.

Serves 4

Arrosto di vitello
Veal Roast with Mustard Sauce and Rosemary Potatoes

For roasts use marbled meat so roast stays juicy. Shoulder or neck pieces are best.

❶ Season veal neck with salt and pepper. Brush on both sides with mustard. Preheat oven to 180 °C.

❷ Coarsely chop onions, carrots and parsley root. Grease roasting pan with olive oil and fill with vegetables, onions and garlic cloves. Place seasoned veal neck on vegetables and add one sprig of thyme and one sprig of rosemary. Pour in one cup of water and roast in pre-heated oven for about 2 hours, keep basting meat with liquid from time to time. After 1 hour of roasting add veal stock and white wine.

❸ In the meantime, peel potatoes, dice and cook in boiling salted water until al dente. Drain in a colander and dry on kitchen towel.

❹ Remove veal roast from pan. Pass sauce through a sieve, bring to a boil and season with salt and pepper. Depending upon taste, use some cold-stirred cornflour and use to bind sauce. You can also use cold butter.

❺ Finely chop remaining rosemary needles. Sauté potatoes in hot olive oil until golden brown and season with salt, pepper and rosemary needles.

❻ Slice veal roast and serve with rosemary potatoes, vegetables and sauce.

Serves 4

1 kg veal neck, bones removed
Salt
Freshly ground black pepper
3 tablespoons mustard, medium-hot
1 onion, peeled
2 carrots, peeled
2 parsley roots, peeled
6 garlic cloves, unpeeled and pressed
2 sprigs of thyme
2 sprigs of rosemary
1/2 l veal stock
1/4 l white wine
500 g potatoes
Olive oil for sautéing

Skewered Sautéed Quails with Bay Leaves and Bacon

This delicious meal should be savoured among good friends, since quails taste best when eaten with the fingers.

❶ Rinse quails with cold water and pat dry with kitchen paper.

❷ Cut baguette into 6 slices of about 2 cm each. Cut off rind and gristles from bacon and slice diagonally into slices as thick as a finger. Preheat oven to 190 °C.

❸ Rub inside and outside of quails with salt and pepper and stuff with fresh rosemary and parsley.

❹ Weave bacon, bay leaves, slices of bread and quails in that order onto 2 large wooden skewers.

❺ Heat olive oil and 1 tablespoon butter in a skillet and briefly sauté quails on all sides. Roast in preheated oven for about 15 minutes until done. Keep basting quails with cooking liquids.

❻ Remove quails from oven and wrap in aluminium foil. Add poultry or veal sauce to cooking liquids, bring to a boil and bind sauce with 2 tablespoons cold butter. Season with salt, pepper and finely ground juniper berries. Grill quails under high heat from above for 2 minutes and serve with juniper sauce.

Serves 4

4 meaty quails, kitchen-ready

1/2 baguette

150 g thick bacon in 1 piece

Salt

Freshly ground black pepper

1 sprig of rosemary

Some sprigs of flat-leaf parsley

1/2 bunch of bay leaves

1 tablespoon olive oil

3 tablespoons unsalted butter

1/4 l brown veal or poultry sauce

3 juniper berries

12. Desserts

Fresh Figs with Zabaione and Amaretti

4 fresh figs

4 tablespoons sugar

100 ml Port wine

1 teaspoon unsalted butter

2 small bay leaves

2 tablespoons honey

100 ml Vin Santo

A pinch of cinnamon

2 egg yolks

12 Amaretti

If you are only familiar with dried figs, you have to try them fresh. These wonderful fruits are harvested twice a year. They are in season at the beginning of the summer and during the late summer months and can be purchased fresh at the farmers' market.

❶ Cut an x in the top of the figs and slightly press them apart. Caramelise 2 tablespoons sugar in a pot until lightly browned. Add Port wine and allow sauce to thicken. Preheat oven to 180 °C.

❷ Place figs in lightly buttered dish and pour Port wine sauce over figs. Add bay leaves, drizzle with honey and bake in preheated oven for about 10 minutes.

❸ In the meantime, stir together Vin Santo, remaining sugar, cinnamon and egg yolks in the top of a double boiler. Place over boiling water, stirring continuously with a whisk until mixture is white and foamy.

❹ Arrange figs with zabaione on plates and sprinkle with coarsely grated amaretti.

Serves 4

Pere al forno
Pears Baked in the Oven with Apricots

Depending on your taste, you can combine "pere al forno" with any fruit you like. This is just a suggestion. Vanilla sauce, vanilla or walnut ice cream or just lightly whipped cream go well with this dessert.

Serves 4-6

8 small pears

1/2 l white wine

Peel of 1/2 lemon, organically grown

Peel of 1/2 organically grown orange

Juice of 1 orange

1 cinnamon stick

2 cloves

1 vanilla pod

2 tablespoons brown sugar

2 tablespoons honey

12 apricots, dried

100 g cream

1 tablespoon confectioners' sugar

❹ 15 minutes before they are done, brush pears with honey, add apricots and bake until done.

❺ Lightly whip cream and 1 tablespoon confectioners' sugar. Arrange pears with apricots and cream in deep plates or little bowls.

❶ Peel pears, leaving a few strips of peel. This looks decorative and the important roughage and vitamins of the peel are preserved. Remove core with an apple corer. Preheat oven to 180 °C.

❷ Stand pears in an oval casserole dish. Bring white wine with orange and lemon peels, orange juice, spices and brown sugar to a boil.

❸ Pour this mixture into the dish with the pears and bake in preheated oven for about 1 hour, basting pears from time to time with the juices.

Panna Cotta with Espresso

Hot espresso adds the right touch to panna cotta. You can also vary this dessert with lightly whipped cream and coffee beans.

❶ Heat cream, sugar and vanilla pod and simmer for about 10 minutes over low heat. In the meantime, soften gelatine in cold water.

❷ Add orange and lemon peel to cream, remove vanilla pod and scrape out vanilla extract into cream. Pat gelatine dry and dissolve in hot cream.

❸ Fill panna cotta into cold-rinsed glasses or molds, cover and refrigerate for 3 to 4 hours.

❹ It is best to serve panna cotta in its containers. Distribute individual portions of hot coffee over panna cotta. Panna cotta tastes even better with a dollop of lightly whipped cream. Hot coffee blends beautifully with cold cream.

Serves 4

500 g cream

100 g sugar

1/2 vanilla pod, cut open

2 sheets unflavoured gelatine

Peel of 1/2 organically grown orange, grated

Peel of 1/2 organically grown lemon, grated

80 ml espresso (about 2 espressi)

Tiramisu

4 egg yolks

100 g sugar

500 g Mascarpone cheese

4 cl Cognac or Brandy

150 ml espresso

   (about 3 espressi)

150 g ladyfingers

Unsweetened cocoa powder

   for dusting

Old and young love this classic dessert of the Italian cuisine. For kids prepare tiramisu without alcohol and replace coffee with hot chocolate. You can also add fresh strawberries or raspberries.

❶ Beat together egg yolks and sugar using a hand blender, until white and creamy. Beat in mascarpone cheese one tablespoon at a time and add 2 cl cognac.

❷ Allow espresso to cool (if you do not have an espresso machine you can use instant espresso powder). Mix espresso with remaining cognac.

❸ Briefly dip half of the ladyfingers into coffee mixture and cover bottom of an oval or square casserole dish. Top with half the mascarpone cream. Add another layer of ladyfingers and finish with mascarpone cream.

❹ Cover tiramisu with clingfilm and refrigerate, preferably overnight, so cream can soak and develop its full flavour. Dust with cocoa powder before serving.

Serves 6-8

Monte Bianco
Maroni Purée with Cream and Chocolate Sauce

❶ Cut an x in maroni shells, place on baking sheet and bake in oven until shells crack. Allow to cool slightly, then peel.

❷ Mix 1/2 l milk with 1/2 l water, add maroni and cook until maroni are soft and liquid has evaporated completely.

❸ Finely purée dry, soft maroni in a food processor. Pass though a fine mesh sieve and finish with lemon and orange peel.

❹ Cook vanilla pudding following the directions on package, allow to cool slightly and fold into maroni purée. Finish with kirsch.

❺ Bring sugar to a boil with a dash of water and cocoa powder, dissolve chopped chocolate coating and allow to cool again. In the end, stir in 200 g cream.

❻ Lightly whip remaining cream and confectioners' sugar with a hand blender. Press maroni purée through spätzle maker and serve with sweetened cream and chocolate sauce.

Serves 4

1.8 kg maroni (Italian chestnuts)
3/4 l milk
A pinch of grated peel of 1
  organically grown lemon
A pinch of grated peel of 1
  organically grown orange
1/2 package vanilla pudding
powder
A dash of kirsch
60 g sugar
1 tablespoon unsweetened
  cocoa powder
100 g semi-sweet chocolate icing
300 g cream
1 heaped tablespoon
  confectioners' sugars

Zuppa Romana

❶ Beat egg yolks with 40 g sugar into a white foamy mixture. Mix remaining sugar with 50 g cornstarch. Beat egg whites and salt until stiff peaks form, then add sugar mixture one tablespoon at a time while beating continuously. Preheat oven to 210 °C.

❷ Mix flour and remaining cornstarch together and sift. Fold one third of egg white mixture into beaten egg mixture, then work in remaining egg whites and flour mixture. Brush biscuit dough onto baking sheet lined with parchment paper and bake in preheated oven for 10 minutes until golden brown. Mix some cornstarch and sugar together and sprinkle over biscuit. Turn out onto kitchen towel and carefully remove parchment paper.

❸ For the cream, soften gelatine in cold water. Mix 3 tablespoons of cold milk with pudding powder, then stir in sugar and egg yolks as well. Bring remaining milk to a boil and add vanilla extract and lemon peel. Work stirred pudding powder into milk, bring to a boil and cook for 2 minutes, stirring constantly. Pat gelatine dry, dissolve in hot liquid and pass through a sieve.

❹ Set bowl with vanilla cream into another bowl filled with ice cubes and stir cream until cold. Whip cream, stir in some cold vanilla cream and fold into rest of vanilla cream. Cut biscuit in half and place into a square dish. Mix all ingredients for soaking liquid together. Lightly drizzle biscuit with liquid. Spread vanilla cream onto biscuit and arrange dried cherries onto cream. Cover with biscuit, drizzle once more with liquid and chill. Whip cream with sugar before serving. Spread a thick layer of whipped cream onto biscuit and garnish with caramelised fruits.

Serves 6

For biscuit:

5 egg yolks

140 g sugar

6 egg whites

80 g cornstarch

100 g flour

A pinch of salt

380 ml milk

70 g sugar

For cream:

4 sheets unflavoured gelatine

400 ml milk

25 g vanilla pudding powder

70 g sugar

4 egg yolks

Extract of 1/2 vanilla pod

Grated peel of 1/2 lemon,
   organically grown

200 g cream

1 small jar of sour cherries, 250 g

For soaking liquid:

120 ml Alchermes
   (Italian liqueur)

50 ml Martini bianco

30 ml Jamaica rum

50 g sugar water (25 g sugar
   cooked with 25 g water)

50 ml sour cherry juice

50 ml Amarena cherry juice

200 g cream

1 tablespoon sugar

250 g caramelised fruits,
   chopped

Moscato Jelly with Strawberries

Juice of 1 orange

Juice of 1 lemon

2 tablespoons sugar

4 sheets of unflavoured gelatine

1/4 l dry white wine

1/4 l Moscato d'Asti
   (sweet Italian wine)

250 g strawberries

2 tablespoons confectioners'
   sugar

A dash of Grand Marnier

This jelly is a great idea if you are hosting a larger summer party, since it can be prepared well in advance and after it's chilled it tastes very refreshing. It can be varied as desired with any fruits in season, e.g. peaches, apricots or mixed wild berries.

❶ Bring orange and lemon juices with sugar to a boil and cook until it has a syrupy consistency. Soak gelatine in cold water.

❷ Add white wine to orange-lemon syrup, then pour in 1/8 l Moscato d'Asti. Bring to a boil once.

❸ Pat gelatine dry and dissolve in the hot liquid. To chill, set in a bowl filled with ice cubes.

❹ Clean strawberries, cut into quarters and marinate with confectioners' sugar and a dash of Grand Marnier. Fill individual strawberry portions into glasses.

❺ Stir remaining Moscato into mixture that is about to jelly, fill into glasses on top of the strawberries and chill. As a last touch, finish with one scoop of lemon or mango sorbet.

Serves 4

13. Cooking glossary

Glossary of technical and foreign language cooking terms

baking, roasting

Cooking food in the oven in a heat-resistant dish, in a baking tin (pan) or on a baking (cookie) sheet. The food is cooked by the hot air of a conventional or a fan oven (a fan oven the same cooking effect is achieved with a lower temperature; see the maker's manual). The temperature most commonly used is 180 °C (350°F), Gas Mark 4, which is ideal for cakes, biscuits (cookies), tarts, flans, roasts, fish and poultry. For puff pastry, soufflés and gratins the temperature should be between 200 °C (400°F), Gas mark 6 and 220 °C (425°F), Gas mark 7. More delicate food such as fish, veal and some poultry may need a lower heat, from 150 °C (300°F), Gas mark 2 to 160 °C (325°F), Gas mark 3.

As a rule of thumb, the lower the temperature, the longer the cooking time.

bain-marie

A container of hot water in which or over which food is gently cooked. It may be a rectangular pan in which pans are placed, but in the domestic kitchen it usually takes the form of a double boiler, a saucepan with a smaller pan fitting over it. It can be improvised satisfactorily by using a bowl over a saucepan containing about 2.5 cm/1 inch of hot water.

A bain-marie is used when it is essential not to overheat what is being cooked. It is used for processes such as melting chocolate, and for cooking sauces or puddings containing cream or eggs. For instance, to make a chocolate mousse, the egg whites are beaten stiff over a warm bain-marie. This makes a particularly airy, light yet firm mousse. A bain-marie is also indispensable for making a successful Hollandaise or Béarnaise sauce. The egg yolks are slowly heated while being stirred until they reach the correct consistency, so that they combine with the melted butter whisked into it little by little.

barding

Covering very lean meat such as saddle of venison, pheasant or saddle of hare with slices of bacon, secured with kitchen string. This ensures that the meat remains juicy and does not dry out, while also adding a pleasant flavour to the meat.

basting

Spooning liquid over food while it is being roasted. Normally the cooking juices are used, but butter, wine, stock (broth) or plain water can be used as well. This constant basting and 'looking after' the meat ensures that it remains juicy and does not dry out. The basting liquid acquires a very intense flavour.

beurre manié

Kneaded butter, used to thicken casseroles and sauces. Equal amounts of flour and butter are kneaded together and added as small knobs into boiling liquid while stirring constantly. This thickening agent has a delicious buttery taste and it is easy to handle because the butter and flour are mixed before being adding to the liquid, reducing the risk of lumps forming in the course of cooking.

blanching

Cooking vegetables such as spinach, leeks and carrots briefly in fast-boiling water. It is important to refresh the vegetables by plunging them in ice-cold water immediately afterwards. This ensures that the vegetables remain crisp and retain their original colour. After blanching, the vegetables are heated in hot stock (broth) or butter before serving.

blini

Pancake (crepe) made of a Russian batter using buckwheat flour, fried in a special small frying pan (skillet) about 15 cm (6 in) in diameter. Wheat flour is often added to the buckwheat flour so that it binds more easily. Blinis are usually served with caviar. They are also delicious with braised meat and game.

boiling

Cooking in liquid that is boiling. The process is synonymous with the concept of cooking. The food is cooked in a large amount of water and the agitation of the liquid will prevent the ingredients sticking to each other. So long as the water is boiling, the temperature will be 100 °C (212°F) for the whole of the cooking time.

bouquet garni

A small bundle of various fresh herbs (usually parsley, thyme and bay leaves), tied together and cooked with the food. The bouquet garni is removed before serving.

braising

This refers to a method of cooking which combines frying, simmering and steaming. First the food is seared in hot oil or fat on all sides. This seals the meat, forming a thin crust; this also forms roasting matter on the bottom of the pan which is very important for the colour and flavour of the sauce. Liquid is then added to the meat, the pan is sealed with a lid and the food is slowly braised in a preheated oven. The method is also good for vegetable and fish dishes. It is excellent for less tender, strongly flavoured cuts of meat such as oxtail, goulash, braising steak or stewing lamb.

breadcrumbs

Dried white crumbs, made from stale bread without the crust. They are used in stuffing mixtures or to coat fish, poultry or other meats such as lamb chops.

brunoise

Finely diced vegetables or potatoes.

canapé

Small, bite-sized pieces of bread with various toppings such as smoked salmon, foie gras, caviar, smoked duck breast, ham and so on. They are served as an appetizer.

carcass

The carcass of poultry used in the preparation of chicken stock (broth). Fish bones are used in a similar way to make fish stock (broth).

carving

Cutting meat or poultry into slices or small pieces for serving. It is a good idea to carve on a carving board with a groove for the juices, using a special carving knife.

casserole

A large heat-resistant cooking pot usually made of cast iron or earthenware, excellent for slow-cooked dishes braises and stews such as oxtail and game ragout. Because of the casserole's large surface area and the lengthy cooking time, the meat is able to release it full flavour. Casseroles may be round or oval, the latter shape being ideally suited for long-shaped pieces of meat such as leg of lamb, rolled cuts of meat or a chicken.

célestine

Fine strips of pancake (crepe) added to soup as a garnish.

chiffonade

Finely cut strips of lettuce, often served with shrimp cocktail.

chinois

Conical strainer or sieve used to strain sauces and soups.

clarification

The removal of cloudy matter from soups, stock (broth) or jelly with lightly beaten egg white. The egg white attracts all the foreign particles which cause the cloudiness and can then be easily removed. The operation is carried out as follows. A lightly beaten egg white is added to some lean minced (ground) beef and chopped vegetables and a few ice cubes are stirred in. The mixture is added to the stock (broth), which should also be well chilled. Heat up while stirring constantly. The egg white begins to thicken at 70 °C (160°F) and in the process it attract all the impurities in the stock (broth). The stock (broth) becomes clear while developing a very intense flavour, as a result of the beef and vegetables. Fish and vegetable stock (broth) can also be clarified in the same way; in these cases the meat is omitted.

coating

The operation of pouring sauce over vegetables, meat or fish.

It also describes the technique of covering slices of meat and fish with beaten egg and breadcrumbs before frying them in hot oil. This gives the food a crisp coating while keeping the inside moist and juicy.

concassée

Blanched, peeled, quartered and de-seeded tomatoes, finely chopped. The term may also be applied to herbs.

consommé

Simple soup made of meat or chicken stock (broth), sometimes garnished. When clarified, it is known as clear or 'double' consommé. Cold consommé is often a jelly.

cream soup, velouté soup

Cream soups are thickened with béchamel sauce. Velouté soups are thickened with an egg and cream mixture. The soup should not be brought back to the boil after the mixture has been added to because the egg yolk would curdle.

crêpes

Thin pancakes made from a batter consisting of milk, flour and eggs. The pancakes are cooked slowly in a frying pan (skillet) until golden. They can be served as a dessert, plain with a sprinkling of sugar and lemon juice, or spread or filled with jam or chocolate. They can also be served as a savoury dish, stuffed with vegetable or other fillings.

deep-frying

The process of cooking food by immersion in hot fat. When the food is cooked and crisp, it is removed from the fat or oil in its basket or with a skimming ladle and left to drain thoroughly on kitchen paper. Because hot oil or fat often spatters it is vital to be extremely careful and avoid the risk of fire. An electric chip pan with an adjustable thermostatically-controlled temperature control is an excellent idea not only because it is safer but it also creates much less of a smell. Peeled potatoes cut into chips (sticks) or slices, shrimps and vegetables in batter are ideal for deep-frying, while deep-fried semolina dumplings are delicious served in soup. Deep-frying is also used for sweet dishes such as doughnuts and apple fritters.

duxelles

Garnish or stuffing consisting of finely chopped mushrooms sweated with diced onions and herbs.

forcemeat or stuffing

Finely chopped meat or fish used to stuff eggs, meat, pasta and so on. It can make a dish in its own right, as in the case of meat balls and quenelles, for example. It is also used as a basis for terrines and pâtés such as deer terrine or wild boar pâté.

filleting

The operation of cutting off the undercut of beef sirloin or similar cuts of pork (tenderloin), veal or lamb; removing the breasts of poultry from the carcass; or cutting the flesh of fish in strip-like pieces from the backbone.

flamber

Pouring spirits (such as brandy, rum or Grand Marnier) over food and setting light to it. The process is used with both savoury and sweet dishes, such as Crêpes Suzette. The spirits need to be warmed slightly first.

fleurons

Small pieces of puff pastry baked into various shapes such as flowers, little ships or shrimps. They are served with fish dishes in a sauce or with chicken fricassée.

flouring

The coating of pieces of fish or meat with flour before frying. This forms a tasty crust round the meat or fish which will be particularly juicy as a result.

frying

Frying is the process of cooking food in hot fat. The best fats and oils for frying are therefore ones that can be heated to a high temperatures such as sunflower oil, clarified butter or goose fat. When butter is used, a little oil is often added to raise the temperature it will reach without burning. Some cuts of meat such as beef steaks or pork cutlets may be fried in a non-stick griddle pan without any fat.

gazpacho

Cold Spanish vegetable soup made with fresh tomatoes, cucumbers, garlic and fresh herbs. It is particularly delicious on a hot summer's day.

glazing

Creating a glossy surface on vegetables, meat, fish or puddings. A suitable stock (broth), the cooking juices, a light caramel, jelly, hot jam or icing is poured over the food in question.

gnocchi

Small dumplings, originally Italian, made from potato, semolina or bread flour, depending on the region, poached briefly in boiling water.

gratiné

Baking dishes under a very high top heat until a brown crust has formed. The ideal topping is grated cheese, breadcrumbs or a mixture of the two.

grilling (broiling)

Cooking with intense radiant heat, provided by gas, electricity or charcoal, the latter giving the food a particularly delicious flavour. The food is cooked on a grid without fat, and grilling (broiling) is therefore particularly good for people who are calorie conscious. Meat, fish, poultry and even vegetables can be cooked in this way.

healthy eating

A well-balanced, varied diet based on wholesome, nutritious foods in the right proportion. Ingredients recommended include wholemeal (wholewheat) products, organic meat, fish and poultry and fresh fruit and vegetables.

julienne

Peeled vegetables cut into thin sticks, the length and thickness of matchsticks. They are cooked in butter or blanched and used as a garnish for soup, fish, meat or poultry dishes.

jus

The name given to cooking juices produced during roasting. It is also to describe brown stock (broth) prepared from various kinds of meat.

kaltschale

Literally 'cold cup', this is a cold sweet soup made with fruit and wine. The fruit, for instance raspberries, melon and strawberries, is finely puréed with lemon juice and wine if so desired to which fresh herbs are added. It is important that it is served chilled.

larding needle

Special needle for pulling lardons (strips of pork fat) through lean meat to keep it moist and make it more tender.

marinade

A mixture based on vinegar, lemon juice, buttermilk or yoghurt, with onions and other vegetables, spices and herbs. Meat or fish is steeped in the mixture for several hours to make it tender and enhance its flavour. Marinades can be also used for dressing salads or for marinating meat that is already tender. Meat marinades give sauces a particularly delicious flavour because they have absorbed the various flavours from the herbs, vegetables and spices.

marinating

Steeping meat or fish in a liquid containing salt, wine, vinegar, lemon juice or milk, and flavourings such as herbs and spices. Marinating has a tenderizing effect on the food and also improves the flavour because of the various ingredients added to the marinade. In addition, marinating also has a preserving effect on meat or fish so that it keeps longer. For instance, raw salmon may be marinated in salt, sugar, herbs and spices.

minestrone

Classic Italian vegetable soup using a wide variety of vegetables, the selection depending on the region and the season. However, pasta and beans are essential ingredients.

mirepoix

Finely diced vegetables, often with the addition of bacon and herbs, fried in butter and used as basis for sauces.

muffins

Round, flat rolls made with yeast dough and baked. In America, muffins are sweet rolls using baking powder as a raising agent, made in special muffin pans. There are many varieties, made for instance with blueberries, raspberries, red currants or chocolate.

pie

A sweet or savoury dish baked in a pastry shell with a pastry top. It is made in a pie tin (pan) with a slanting edge 5 cm (2 in) high. The lid of dough should have a small opening in the middle so that the steam can escape, preventing the inside from becoming distended.

ramekin or cocotte

A small, round oven-proof china or earthenware dish in which individual portions are cooked and served.

reducing

Concentrating a liquid by boiling it so that the volume is reduced by evaporation. It increases the flavour of what is left. Strongly reducing a sauce gives a particularly tasty result with a beautiful shine.

refreshing

Dipping food, particularly vegetables, briefly in cold water after cooking to preserve the colour, mineral content and vitamins. The cooked vegetables or other items are then drained in a colander.

roasting

See baking.

roux

A mixture of butter and flour used to thicken sauces. The mixture is made by melting butter and stirring in flour. This is then diluted with milk or stock (broth) and cooked for at least 15 minutes while stirring constantly. For a dark roux, the flour is cooked until it turns brown before liquid is added. Because this reduces the thickening quality of the flour, the amount of flour should be increased.

royale

A custard-like cooked egg garnish. Milk and eggs are stirred together, seasoned, poured into small buttered moulds and poached in a bain-marie at 70–80 °C (160–180°F). They are then turned out and diced.

salamander

Electric appliance used to caramelize or brown the top of certain dishes. It is comparable to a grill, which is normally used as a substitute.

sauté

Cooking food in fat in a frying pan (skillet). Small, uniform pieces of meat, fish, chopped vegetables or sliced potatoes are cooked in a pan while being tossed to prevent them sticking. In this way all sides of the food are cooked.

simmering

Cooked food in liquid over a low heat, just below boiling point. This method of cooking is often used for making soups and sauces since it makes the food tender and enables it to develop its full aroma.

soufflé

Particularly light, aerated dish made with beaten egg white which may be sweet or savoury. A meal which finishes with a mouth-watering chocolate soufflé will always be remembered with great pleasure.

soup bones

Meat bones, poultry carcass or fish bones used in making stock (broth). These are very important ingredients because they give an intense flavour to the stock (broth). Smooth beef and veal bones are ideal, but the marrow bone has the most flavour. It is important that the bones should purchased from a reliable butcher and come from a guaranteed source so as to avoid any risk of BSE (mad cow disease).

steaming

Cooking over a boiling water so that the food is out of contact with the liquid and cooks in the steam. To achieve this, the food is cooked in a perforated container over lightly boiling water or stock (broth). This method of cooking ensures that vegetables keep their flavour particularly well. They remain crisp and full of taste. Fish too can be cooked in this way without any additional fat but simply with herbs and spices. Steaming is particularly good for the preparation of low-calorie dishes for people who must follow a low-fat diet for reasons of health. But it will also appeal to everyone who loves the pure, genuine flavour of food.

stock (broth)

The flavoured liquid base of soups and sauces. Basic meat stocks (broths) for soups and sauces are made by simmering meat and bones of veal, beef, game, poultry or fish for several hours. As the liquid simmers gently, the constantly forming foam is periodically removed with a skimming ladle. When the stock (broth) has cooled down, the layer of fat can be removed so that the stock (broth) becomes light and clear. Vegetable stock (broth) is made in a similar way by boiling vegetables and herbs

straining

Filtering solid matter from liquids or draining liquids from raw or cooked food. Soups, sauces and stock (broth) are poured or pressed through a fine sieve. In the case of a stock (broth) the sieve may be lined with a coarse cloth.

string

Kitchen string is used to truss poultry or to tie a joint of meat so that it keeps its shape while being cooked.

suprême

Breast of chicken or game. The name refers to the best part of the bird, which is always prepared with the greatest care.

sweating

Frying the food lightly in a little fat in a pan over moderate heat, so that it softens but does not brown.

tartlet

Small tart made from short crust or puff pastry with a sweet or savoury filling.

tenderizing

Making tough meat tender by beating it. The meat is placed between two sheets of foil and beaten with a mallet or the bottom of a small pan until it has become thin. It is used for roulades, veal escalopes and so on.

thickening

The addition of a substance to a sauce or soup to thicken it. There are several common methods. Flour may be added and stirred continuously until the liquid thickens. A variation is to mix butter and flour as a roux to which the liquid is slowly added, again stirring constantly. Alternatively egg yolk or cream can be stirred into the liquid to make an emulsion. On no account must it be allowed to boil or it will curdle. After the yolk has been stirred into the sauce or soup, it must not be cooked any more or it will curdle.

timbale

Mould lined with pastry, blind-baked and filled with meat, fish or other ingredients in a sauce, baked in the oven or cooked in a bain-marie.

trimming

The removal of connective tissue and fat from all kind of meats. The off-cuts are used in the preparation of stock (broth) and sauces. It is important to use a very sharp knife, held flat against the meat so as not to remove too much meat in the process.

turning

Forming vegetables and potatoes into decorative shapes, such as balls, ovals or spirals. This is carried out using a small knife with a crescent-shaped blade.

zest

The thin outer rind of oranges or lemons, used for its flavour and fragrance. It is cut from the pith in thin strips, using a zester.

Herbs and spices

agar

Thickening agent made from dried algae from Asia. It is used as a vegetable gelling agent, for instance in the manufacturing of blancmange powder, jelly or processed cheese. Agar only dissolves in very hot liquid and has highly gelatinous properties. It is therefore important to follow the instructions very carefully. It is particularly useful in vegetarian cuisine where it is an alternative to gelatine, which is made from beef bones. Agar is often combined with other thickening agents such as carob bean flour because it is very indigestible. This makes it a much more effective thickening agent.

allspice

These brown berries are grown in tropical countries, particularly Jamaica. The complex, multi-layered aroma of allspice is at its best when the fresh grains are crushed in a mortar. It is used to season lamb and beef ragouts, sausages, pies and gingerbread.

aniseed

Aniseed is often associated with the delicious aroma of Christmas cakes and pastries. The seed can be used whole, crushed or ground. It is also used in savoury dishes, for instance in the seasoning and marinades of fish and preparation of fish stock (broth). It is the main flavour of alcoholic drinks such as pastis and ouzo.

basil

Basil is undoubtedly the king of all fresh herbs used in the kitchen. It is an aromatic annual herb that plays an important part in a wide variety of dishes. It has a particular affinity with tomatoes and it is used in salads and many Mediterranean dishes.

basil, Thai

Thai basil is an important herb in Thai cuisine, used in baked noodle dishes, sauces and curries. It is available in many shops specialising in eastern food. It is very delicate and should be used as fresh as possible.

bay leaves

The leathery leaves of the bay tree have a spicy, bitter taste which becomes even stronger when dried. It is one of the ingredients of a bouquet garni. The fresh leaves are added to fish, while dried it is an important ingredient of many preserved dishes, such as braised meat marinated in vinegar and herbs, or pickled gherkins.

borage

A herb with hairy leaves and wonderful blue flowers. It has a slightly bitter, tangy taste reminiscent of cucumber and is mainly used in drinks such as Pimms. It is also a good accompaniment to salads, soups, cabbage and meat dishes.

burnet, salad

The leaves must be harvested before the plant flowers. Salad burnet is used in the same way as borage. It is only used fresh since it loses its aroma completely when dried.

caraway

Caraway is the traditional spice used in rich, fatty dishes such as roast pork, sauerkraut, raw cabbage dishes and stews – not simply for its aromatic flavour but also because of its digestive properties. It is added to some cheeses. Whole or ground, it is also used in spiced bread and cakes. Many liqueurs contain caraway because of its digestive properties.

cardamom

After saffron, cardamom is one of the most expensive spices in the world. Removed from the pod, the seeds are used ground. Just a pinch will be enough to add a delicious taste to rice dishes, cakes or gingerbread.

chervil

The fine flavour of chervil will enhance any spring or summer dish. It can be used in salads, soups and fish dishes and it is also very decorative.

chilli peppers

Red or green chilli peppers are hot and add a spicy, aromatic pungency to food. They are available fresh, dried, ground, pickled or in the form of a paste or essence (extract). When using fresh peppers, it is advisable to remove the seeds which are the hottest part. They are especially popular in Central and south-western America, the West Indies and Asia, forming an integral part of many dishes originating in these regions.

chives

This is one of the great traditional cooking herbs which is available throughout the year. Very versatile, chives are sold fresh in bunches and are delicious with fromage frais, bread and butter, scrambled eggs or fresh asparagus. The beautiful blue flowers of the chive plant are very decorative and also delicious, making a great addition with the leaves to any salad in the summer.

cloves

The flower buds of the clove tree have an intensely spicy aroma with a bitter, woody taste. That is why it should be used sparingly. Cloves are used in marinades, red cabbage and braised dishes as well as in mulled wine and many Christmas cakes and buns.

coriander (cilantro)

Coriander seeds have been used for a long time, mainly as a pickling spice and in Oriental dishes. Fresh green coriander leaves (cilantro) have become available in many countries much more recently. Finely chopped, this sweetish spicy herb adds an exotic aroma to many dishes, including guacamole. It should be used with discretion by those who are not used to the taste.

cress

The small-leafed relative of the watercress is slightly less aromatic. It is usually sold as small plants in paper containers or as seeds to grow oneself, often with mustard as the mustard and cress used in elegant sandwiches. Cress is commonly used to garnish egg dishes and salads.

cumin

This classic spice is common in eastern cuisine and is a fundamental ingredient of curry powder and curry pastes. It adds an interesting, exotic flavour to braised dishes such as lamb, kid or beef.

curry powder

Curry powder may be made from as many as 30 spices, including among others turmeric, pepper, cumin, caraway, cloves, ginger and allspice. It is extremely versatile and in addition to its use in curries it can be used in small quantities to add flavour to many meat, fish and poultry dishes.

dill

An annual sweetish aromatic herb, common in northern European cooking but seldom used in Mediterranean dishes. The feathery leaves are used fresh in fish dishes, sauces, with fromage frais, and in vegetable dishes. Cucumber pickles (dill pickles) make use of the leaves and the seeds.

fennel

Fennel leaves have a slight flavour of aniseed and are commonly used with fish. The seeds are sometimes used to season bread. When added to fish dishes and fish stock (broth), the seeds are crushed first.

fines herbes

Classic French combination of herbs, made from parsley, tarragon, chervil, chives, and perhaps thyme, rosemary and other herbs. Fines herbes may be used fresh, dried or frozen. The commonest use is in omelettes.

galangal

A close relative of the ginger family which is much used in south-eastern cuisine. The roots can used fresh, dried, ground or dried.

garam masala

The meaning of this Indian name is 'hot mixture', and it consists of up to 13 spices. It plays an important part in the cooking of India, where it is home-made, so that its composition varies from family to family. Garam masala is available commercially in supermarkets and in shops specialising in Asian food.

garlic

Cooking without garlic is unimaginable to anyone who loves and enjoys the pleasures of the Mediterranean. Freshly chopped, it enhances salads and cold sauces, roasts, stews, braised and grilled (broiled) dishes all benefit from the addition of garlic. Another popular use is in garlic bread.

gelatine

Gelatine is a thickening agent made from beef bones. Leaf gelatine must be soaked thoroughly in plenty of cold water for five or ten minutes before using it. It is then squeezed well and diluted in warm water. A special technique is needed when using gelatine in cream-based dishes. A few spoonfuls of cream are stirred into the gelatine. This mixture is then stirred into the rest of the cream. In this way lumps will be avoided.

ginger

The juicy roots of ginger have a sharp fruity aroma. Ginger adds an interesting, exotic touch to both savoury and sweet dishes. Because ginger freezes very well it can be kept for a long time without losing any of its flavour. A piece can be broken off whenever it is needed.

lavender

The taste of lavender is bitter and spicy. It can be used as a seasoning for lamb-based dishes, meat and fish stews and salads. The flowers are particularly decorative.

lovage

Lovage has a celery-like taste and both the stems and the leaves can be used in soup, salads and sauces. The finely chopped leaves are sometimes added to bread dumplings, and to the stuffing for breast of veal to which it adds a particularly delicate flavour.

marjoram

Sweet marjoram is a popular herb with a distinctive aroma. It can be used either fresh and dried, but like almost all herbs it is best when it is fresh. Marjoram is delicious in potato soups and omelettes. Pot marjoram is a hardier form with a stronger flavour, so it is advisable not to use too much.

mint

Mint is delicious as mint tea and also in puddings such a mint ice cream, and in drinks. It is part of many soups, salads and meat dishes, and is often added to potatoes and peas. Mint sauce is served with lamb. Mint leaves are also often used as decoration.

mugwort

This is a variety of wormwood. It grows in the wild and the sprigs should be collected just before the plants flower. They can also be dried for later use. Mugwort is popular with roast goose and game.

mustard seeds

Mustard seeds are one of the most important ingredients in pickled vegetables such as gherkins, courgettes (zucchini), pumpkin, mixed pickles and pickled cocktail onions. They are often used too in braised beef, marinated in vinegar and herbs.

nasturtiums

Nasturtium flowers are very decorative and the leaves are delicious, their sharp, peppery taste adding a spicy touch to any salad.

nutmeg

Grated nutmeg is delicious in soups, stews, potato purée and cabbage. It is a also a traditional seasoning in Christmas cakes and confectionery. It tastes best when freshly grated.

oregano

Also known as wild marjoram, oregano is much used in Italian cuisine. It is essential in many dishes such as pizzas, pasta with tomato sauce and aubergine (egg plant) dishes. In the case of pizzas it is best to use dried oregano because the fresh leaves become brown in the very strong heat of the hot oven, thus losing much of their flavour.

parsley

The most popular of all herbs, two varieties are common, one with curly leaves and the other with smooth leaves. But it is not only the leaves that are used; the roots too are full of flavour and are delicious added to soups and sauces. Parsley has a deliciously fresh aroma and a strong taste. It is also extremely rich in vitamins and minerals, so it is an important herb for use in winter.

pepper

Black pepper and white pepper have different tastes as well as looking different. Black pepper is obtained by harvesting the unripe fruit, while white pepper is the ripe fruit which is peeled before being dried. White pepper is milder, more delicate in taste and not as sharp as black.

purslane

The green, fleshy leaves can be used raw in salads or used as a vegetable in its own right as in the Far East. The delicious leaves have a slightly salty flavour.

rosemary

Rosemary has a particular affinity with lamb, which is often roasted with a few sprigs. It is particularly popular in France where it is used in many dishes such as soups, potatoes, vegetables, meat and fish dishes. Dried, chopped rosemary is one of the ingredients of *herbes de Provence*.

saffron

This bright orange spice is the 'golden' condiment of good cuisine, providing an inimitable flavour and colour. It consists of the dried stigmas of the saffron crocus, and about 4,000 of these are needed for 25 g (1 oz), which accounts for its high cost. But only a small amounts is needed; just a few filaments or a tiny pinch of ground saffron will be enough to add a very special taste to bouillabaisse, paella or risotto.

sage

The sharp, slightly bitter taste of sage is ideal with roast goose or roast lamb. Often used in sausages, it is also one of the most important ingredients of the Italian classic 'Saltimbocca' (veal escalope with sage and Parma ham). The fresh leaves are delicious dipped in batter and fried.

savory

Savory is a peppery herb used in many bean-based dishes and also in stews and casseroles. The stem is cooked in the stew while the young shoots are chopped up and added to the dish just before the end of the cooking time.

star anise

This is the small star-shaped seed of the Chinese aniseed, native to China. The flavour is a little more bitter than aniseed itself. It can be used for baking and cooking and adds a delicious flavour to leg of lamb and dried apricots or in sweet and sour beef stew. It can also be used in puddings such as apple or quince compote.

tamarind

The pods contains a very sour juice which is much used in Indian and Thai cooking. Dishes such as baked fish with tamarind sauce, cherry tomatoes and fresh ginger are quite delicious.

tarragon

Tarragon has a delicate, spicy flavour. It can be used on its own as in tarragon vinegar or tarragon mustard, in Béarnaise as well as in a wide range of poultry and fish dishes. It is also excellent when combined with other herbs such as chervil, chives and parsley. The variety to be used is French tarragon. Russian tarragon grows easily from seed but has little flavour.

thyme

Like rosemary, this sweetish spicy herb is particularly good with Mediterranean food. It is an essential part of a bouquet garni and one of the main ingredients of *herbes de Provence*. Thyme will add a special touch to any dish, whether meat, fish, poultry or vegetables.

turmeric

Turmeric is much used in oriental cuisine. It is one of the basic ingredients of curry powder, Thai fish and meat curries and Indian rice dishes. It has an intense, yellow colour, but it should not be confused with saffron which has a very different taste.

vanilla

The fruit pods (beans) of the tropical vanilla orchid tree add a delicious aroma to cakes, puddings, ice cream, confectionery and so on. In cakes it is best to use vanilla essence (extract) while to make ice-cream and rice pudding, the crushed pod (bean) is added to the hot liquid si tha it releases its delicate aroma. Vanilla sugar is made by leaving a pod (bean) in a container of sugar.

wasabi

Very sharp green radish usually available as a paste or powder. It used to season sushi and many other Japanese dishes. It is important not to add too much. Wasabi is usually served separately as well so that every one can mix it to the sharpness they like.

watercress

Watercress grows in the wild but it should not be eaten in case it contains paraites. Cultivated watercress is readily available. This is grown in watercress beds with pure water of the correct temperature running through them. Watercress has a hot, spicy taste and is delicious on its own, on bread and butter, in green salads, in cream soups, in risottos and in potato salad.

woodruff, sweet

Smelling of new-mown hay, sweet woodruff is only available in May, and it is therefore best-known as the essential ingredient in the aromatic drinks of traditional Maytime celebrations, such as the May wine cup in Germany and May wine punch in the United States. It is delicious in desserts, such as fresh strawberries marinated in woodruff, or wine jelly with fruit and fresh woodruff.

14. Index

Subject Index

Fish

Seafood

Beef

Poultry

Rabbit

Braised Rabbit with Tomatoes and
    Artichokes 151

Game

Chestnut-Walnut-Crusted Leg of
    Wild Boar 157
Green Maltagliate with Wild Boar Ragoût
    and Porcini Mushrooms 95

Goat

Stuffed Baby Goat with Stinging Nettles
    and Potatoes 162

Viscera

Trippa alla parmigiana - Tripe in Tomato
    Sauce and Parmesan 167
Veal Liver with Raisins and Pine Nuts 144

Sausage and Ham

Chickpea Soup with Pancetta 71
Crespelle with Spicy Salsiccia-Onion
    Sauce 109
Pumpkin Gnocchi with Salsiccia and
    Fennel Seeds 99
Spinach-Feta-Dumplings with Sage-
    Parma-Ham-Butter 96
Tramezzini with Scrambled Eggs
    and Ham 51

Lamb

Roasted Saddle of Lamb Wrapped in
    Bacon with Leek and Truffles 163
Sautéed Lamb Cutlets with Tomatoes
    and Rosemary Oil 164

Vegetables

Bagna caôda - Vegetable Fondue with
    Hot Anchovy Sauce 54
Caramelised Carrots with Raisins
    and Mint 59
Cream of Rice Soup with Green Beans 75
Crespelle Filled with Riccotta and
    Radicchio 110
Crespelle Filled with Spinach and
    Tomatoes 107
Fresh Figs with Parma Ham and
    Grissini 60
Gnocchi with Radicchio, Capers and
    Olives 97
Marinated Vegetables 58
Minestrone with Pasta 75
Peperonata with Garlic 52
Savoy Cabbage Stew with Fontina
    Cheese and Sage 70
Sweet-and-Sour Yellow Onions 59
Zuppa di Pomodori - Tomato Soup
    with Pesto and Garlic Croûtons 68

Polenta

Grilled Polenta with Cherry Tomatoes
    and Fontina Cheese 113
Liquid Polenta with Gorgonzola Cheese
    and Butter 114
Polenta with Chanterelle Mushrooms and
    Rosemary Butter 114

Risotto

Prosecco Risotto with Sautéed
    Porcini Mushrooms 117
Pumpkin Risotto with Ricotta 119
Spinach Risotto with White Truffles 118

Pasta

Bevette all'amatriciana - Pasta with
    Onion Sauce and Chopped Egg 84
Bucatini alla Carbonara 103
Cannelloni 27
Cannelloni Stuffed with Walnuts, Robiola
    and Poultry Liver 83
Cannelloni with Melted Tomatoes and
    Cheese Sauce 80
Capellini aglio e olio - Capellini with
    Garlic and Olive Oil 78
Green Pasta Dough 22
Lasagne with Meat Sauce and
    Mozzarella 82
Linguine with Diced Eggplant 88
Orecchiette with Broccoli and Red
    Onions 87
Pappardelle with Pepper Sauce 98
Pasta dough 22
Ravioli 24
Ravioli with Sage Butter 89
Spaghetti Aurora - Spaghetti with
    Cream of Tomato Sauce 101
Spaghetti Bolognese 90
Spaghetti with Prawns, Cucumber
    and Peperoncini 98
Tortellini 26
Tortelloni 26

Salad

Insalata Caprese - Mozzarella with
    Tomatoes and Fried Basil 57
Panzanella - Bread Salad 63
Raw Artichoke Salad with Grated
    Parmesan Cheese 53
Sicilian Orange Salad with Fennel
    and Olives 48

Sauce

Fish Stock 42
Orange Vinaigrette 43
Pesto 28
Poultry Stock 42
Saint Stefano Vinaigrette 43
Seafood Stock 39
Tomato Sauce 44
Tuna Sauce 40
Walnut-Honey Sauce 40

Dessert

Fresh Figs with Zabaione and
    Amaretti 174
Monte Bianco - Maroni Purée with Cream
    and Chocolate Sauce 183
Moscato Jelly with Strawberries 186
Panna Cotta with Espresso 179
Pere al forno - Pears Baked in the Oven
    with Apricots 176
Tiramisu 180
Zuppa Romana 185

alphabetical Index

Concept and Realisation:

FOOD LOOK
KÖLN
NEW
YORK

Text and Recipes: FOOD LOOK, Cologne

Layout and Type: FOOD LOOK, Cologne

Editors: Monika Kellermann and Gertrud Köhn, Munich

Translation: Barbara Sauermann, New York

Photographs: FOOD LOOK, New York

Peter Medilek

Food Styling: FOOD LOOK STUDIO, Cologne

Cover Photograph: Brigitte Sporrer und Alena Hrbkova

Overall Production: Printing Works Appl, Wemding

© 2001 DuMont Buchverlag, Köln

(Dumont monte UK, London)

ISBN 3-7701-7057-1

Printed in Germany